A GREAT WEEKEND IN

BRUSSELS

Brussels,
the secret city

Like the River Senne that flows across it, Brussels is a secret, hidden city full of unexpected sights and attractions. Although it may not reveal its charms at first, it has much to offer, amuse and interest its visitors. Among the capitals of Europe, it remains misunderstood, yet Brussels is a city that'll happily open its heart to you if you're ready to give it the chance.

Home to the Surrealists and the Brueghels, Brussels has a feast of delights on offer.

The Grand-Place and its surrounding area is known as the 'belly of Brussels' – an Art Nouveau jewel, a tower of Babel and the capital of Europe, whose inhabitants both love it and loathe it. You may have to turn a blind eye to the disfiguring building sites and try to forget its chaotic lack of urban planning, which has massacred whole neighbourhoods, but since it gained independence within a divided country, Brussels has only looked forward. People are moving back to the city after a worrying period of desertion and can be found decorating their façades in brilliant colours and filling their window boxes with beautiful flowers. The city centre has been revived by a handful of restaurateurs, fashionable designers and bar-owners, with new and ever more attractive establishments opening every week. Forced to stay inside for most of the year, the people of Brussels, are geniuses when it comes to interior design. The city's Art Nouveau architecture, for which Brussels was famed in the prosperous days of the early 20th century, is once again being appreciated. Victor Horta's house and the Van Eetvelde hotel have recently been restored. A superb Andalusian-style house, which long stood derelict, has been transformed into a cultural centre and the wrought-ironwork on a group of quaint old shops has finally

been re-painted in honour of the arrival of the Musée Instrumental. The city's inhabitants are friendly and hospitable, with barely one million inhabitants in total, and more green space per inhabitant than in any other European city, Brussels is hardly overcrowded. Its dozens of tree-filled parks lend a country air to the capital which many other cities envy. Brussels extends far beyond the area contained within the pentagon formed by its 14th-century ramparts. The 19 'communes', or districts, outside the walls have merged with those inside to such an extent that the uninitiated never notice which part they're in, whether it's Brussels-Ville, Ixelles, Saint-Gilles or Forest. In fact, only the Marolles

born-and-bred inhabitants can truly claim to be from Brussels. These rebellious characters, whose bawdy attitudes are expressed entirely in the local *brusseleir* dialect, are always a tourist attraction at the flea markets. In fact, Brussels has an interesting patchwork of neighbourhoods. From working-class Marolles to aristocratic Sablon, from the tourist centre of Grand-Place to trendy Saint-Géry, you can quickly move from one type of atmosphere to the next. It's also a multicultural, multilingual city, where half of the population are foreign, a great many of them European. In the same street, for example, you'll find an Italian delicatessen, a Greek restaurant, a Spanish *bodega* and a traditional Belgian chip-shop. This diversity makes for a gourmet's paradise, as the restaurants compete to produce the most imaginative combination of cuisines and flavours from around the world. The city is

also an Ali Baba's cave for connoisseurs of antiques and ethnic artefacts. People come from far and wide to comb the bric-a-brac and antique shops for bargains. Once inside these places it's hard to leave without making a purchase. Fashion is also important in Brussels. Designers such as Olivier Strelli, Dries Van Noten, Dirk Bikkembergs as well as Ann Demeulemeester, whose talents have been noticed abroad for a few years now, live and work in the city. Elvis Pompilio conjures up the wildest hats imaginable and the new second-hand dealers excel in the art of turning old into new. Whatever the weather, a night out in the trendy bars and clubs can be hot, but the cafés are where you'll find that image you've had in mind all weekend: the tireless beer-drinker from a Brueghel banquet or one of Magritte's chessplayers. From chocolate to Surrealist art and fashion to secondhand comics, Brussels, once visited, is a city to which you'll want to return, again and again.

How to get there

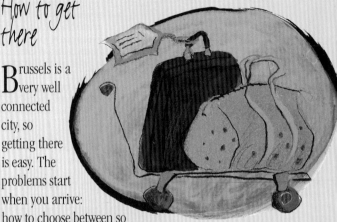

Brussels is a very well connected city, so getting there is easy. The problems start when you arrive: how to choose between so many museums, restaurants and shops? Whether your passion is chocolate, comics, architecture, beer or all of the above, the city that's been called 'the world's best theatre' is at your disposal.

A FEW DATES
TO REMEMBER:

January: Brussels International Film Festival

March: International Fantasy Film Festival

March: Eurantica (antiques market)

Late April-Early May: tours of the Royal Greenhouses in Laeken

May-June: Queen Elisabeth International Musicians' Competition

July: Ommegang (procession and festival in honour of the Holy Roman emperor Charles V (1500-58))

Weekend of 15 August (every other year): floral displays

Early December: Christmas market.

CLIMATE

Given that it rains at least 200 days a year, don't forget to take your mac and your umbrella. The other 165 days could be anything from dull and grey to cold or even very hot. Winters are usually mild and wet, spring is sometimes very pleasant and you may find yourself in the middle of a heatwave in summer. If you're bargain-hunting, remember the sales start on 1 July and 1 January. The main cultural season lasts from September to May, but in the summer music-lovers can enjoy the festivals of Flanders and Wallonia. Find out what's on at the tourist office on Grand-Place (TIB ☎ 00 322 513 8940). There are performances, festivals and exhibitions in Brussels all year round.

HOW TO GET THERE

FLIGHTS FROM THE UK

There are many airlines which fly direct from the UK, so shop around for special deals with budget airlines. It's also worth checking the newspapers as they often offer tokens for cheap ticket deals.

British Airways
☎ 0345 222111
www.british-airways.com
BA offer several direct flights a day from London Heathrow. Journey time is 1 hr 15 mins. There are also on average 2 direct flights a day from London Gatwick, Birmingham, Manchester and Southampton airports. Ticket prices vary according to date, time of travel, ticket class etc. You can also make bookings at the

British Airways Travel Shop based in London on ☎ 0207 434 4700.

Virgin Express
☎ 0207 744 0004
www.virgin-express.com
Direct flights from London

London Heathrow, London City, Sheffield, Manchester, Birmingham, Leeds/Bradford, Glasgow and Edinburgh airports.

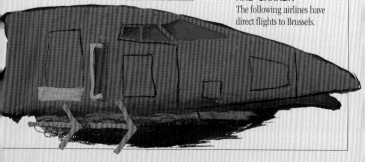

Gatwick, Heathrow and Stansted.

British Midlands
☎ 0870 60 70 555
www.iflybritishmidland.com
Direct flights from London Heathrow, Birmingham and East Midlands airport. Flights from Leeds/Bradford, Manchester, Teeside and Glasgow go via Heathrow.

Sabena
☎ 0208 780 1444
www.sabena.com
Sabena offer on average three direct flights a day from

FROM IRELAND
Aer Lingus
☎ 0208 899 4747 (UK)
☎ 353 1 886 8888 (Ireland)
www.aerlingus.ie
Direct flights from Dublin, Cork, Shannon, Galway and Kerry.

Ryanair
☎ 0906 766 1000 (UK)
☎ 1550 224 499 (Ireland)
www.ryanair.ie
This low cost airline flies direct from Dublin.

Also **Virgin Express** fly from Shannon via London Stansted and **British**

Midlands fly from Dublin via East Midlands airport.

FROM AUSTRALIA AND NEW ZEALAND
Qantas
☎ (02) 9691 3636
🅕 (02) 9691 3339
www.qantas.com.au
Direct flights to London Heathrow and Paris, from where a choice of connecting flights can be made.

There are no direct flights from New Zealand.

Cathay Pacific
www.cathaypacific.com
Offer flights from Auckland to London Heathrow and Paris both via Hong Kong.

Singapore Airlines
☎ (65) 580 7005
www.singaporeair.com
Fly from Auckland via Singapore.

FROM THE USA AND CANADA
The following airlines have direct flights to Brussels.

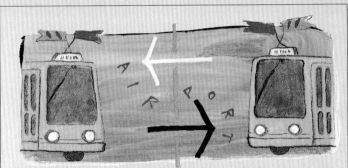

American Airlines
☎ 1-800-433-7300
www.aa.com.

United Airlines
☎ 1-800-241-6522
www.unitedairlines.com.

Delta Airlines
☎ 1-800-241-4141
www.deltaairlines.com.

Air Canada
☎ 1-888-247-2262
www.aircanada.ca
Flights from most major
Canadian airports via London.

Sabena also have daily
flights from New York JFK,
Boston, Chicago and Montreal
airports.

BY TRAIN
Eurostar
☎ 0870 518 6186
www.eurostar.com
The Eurostar runs to Brussels
from London Waterloo or you
can pick it up at Ashford
International station (Kent).
Departures are generally every
2 hrs, with 10 trains a day
during the week and roughly
8 at the weekend. Journey time
from Waterloo is around 2 hrs
40 mins, 1 hr less if travelling
from Ashford. You can book
using a credit card over the
phone or via the internet,
which will allow you to browse
through the online timetables
to help you plan your journey.

BY COACH
Eurolines
☎ 08705 143 219 or
☎ 0990 186186
Eurolines run a coach service
to Brussels from London
Victoria, leaving twice a day, at
10.30am and 10.30pm, 7 days
a week. It takes roughly 8 hrs
and can also be picked up at
Dover.

BY SEA
Hoverspeed
Bookings: ☎ 0870 240 8070
🖷 01304 865 203.
Port and travel information:
☎ 01304 865000
🖷 01304 865 226

INCLUSIVE BREAKS

Tour operators generally offer 2 or 3-day weekend breaks at fixed prices including transport (plane, train or coach) and a choice of various types of hotel. To take advantage of such an offer, you'll have to spend Saturday night in Brussels. If you decide to go for one of these deals, you'll benefit from the lower prices negotiated by the travel agent and you won't have to worry about making all the reservations yourself. It's as well to bear in mind that, luxury hotels aside, the selection of 2 and 3-star hotels in Brussels is for the most part limited to the type of package deal that takes in groups of tourists all year round.

www.hoverspeed.co.uk, email: reservations@hoverspeed.co.uk A hovercraft service runs between Dover and Calais (2 hrs drive from Brussels) leaving every hour on the hour (about 12 departures a day). Journey time is 35 mins. The seacat service runs between Dover and Ostend (1 hrs drive from Brussels) with 5 departures a day, taking 2 hrs. NB: hovercrafts and sea cats do not run in rough weather.

P&O Stena Line
☎ 0870 600 0600 or
☎ 0990 980 980
www.posl.com, email: customer.services@posl.com
Cross-channel ferries every 45 mins from Dover to Calais (every half hour at peak times), taking 75 mins.

P&O North Sea Ferries
Bookings: ☎ 01482 377 177
www.ponsf.com.
Enquiries: ☎ 01482 795141
🖷 01482 706438
email: info.uk@ponsf.com.

Daily ferry service from Hull to Zeebrugge, taking 14 hrs.

SeaFrance
☎ 08705 711 711
www.SeaFrance.com.
The only French ferry company sailing between Dover and Calais, with around 15 departures a day. Journey time is about 90 mins.

FROM THE AIRPORT TO THE CITY CENTRE

Zaventem airport is 14 km/ 9 miles north-east of Brussels. There's a choice of three modes of transport to the city centre. Quickest and cheapest is the train, which gets you to the central station in 20 mins. Departures every 20 mins from 5.30am until 11.45pm from the station in the terminal basement. The ticket office is open from 6.30am to 10pm (BF90 for a single). From the stop outside the airport, bus BZ, run by DE LIJN, has departures at 5 mins past the hour every hour on weekdays. It will take you to the city centre in 30 mins at best. At weekends there's only a bus every two hours.

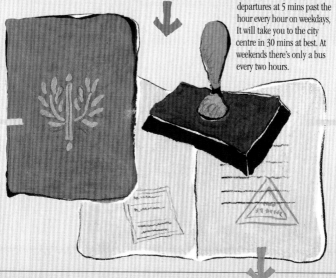

BUDGETING

Life in Brussels isn't as expensive as some European cities, with the possible exception of restaurants. After paying for your hotel and transport you'll need around BF3,600 to 6,000 for restaurants, drinks, excursions, museums and concerts, although some cultural activities are free. Allow between BF500 and 1,200 for a meal including drinks, BF75-200 for a museum, BF50 for a tram ticket, BF40-50 for a coffee or a beer, BF150-200 for a cocktail or a measure of spirits, BF200-500 to get into a club, BF200-500 to see a play or a concert and BF300-450 to take a taxi.

Buy your ticket (BF70) from the driver. You can get a taxi from the airport to your hotel door for about BF1,000. Journey time varies from half to 1 hour.

HIRING A CAR

It may be cheaper to hire a car before you leave. Once in Brussels, you'll find car hire companies offering widely differing rates at both the airport (arrivals hall) and city centre. It's up to you to compare the prices and advantages. Don't forget to ask for the 'weekend' rate and take care when you're parking in the city centre. Any cars parked illegally are soon towed away to the pound.

Europcar offers the best 'weekend' rates
☎ 0 803 358 358
In Brussels:
Gare du Midi: ☎ 522 95 73
Airport: ☎ 721 05 92.

FORMALITIES

EU nationals, including children under 16, must have a valid identity card or passport. A passport that has expired within the last five years is also acceptable. If you're travelling from the U.S.A, Canada, Australia or New Zealand, you'll require a valid passport. You'll only require a visa if you're staying for three months or longer.

CUSTOMS

Customs officers make only routine border checks on EU nationals, however, the traffic in drugs from the Netherlands means you may be searched if you travel by train. Duty-free purchases are available only between Belgium and non-EU countries since the abolition of duty-free between EU countries in June 1999. Duty-free allowances are 200 cigarettes or 50 cigars, 2l of wine, 1l of alcohol of more than 22°, 2l of less than 22°, 50cl of perfume, 25cl of eau de toilette and 500gm/ 1.1lbs of coffee. The importation of firearms, amunition, knives, swords, etc., is illegal.

INSURANCE

The fixed insurance deals offered by tour operators usually cover the cost of repatriation, but not cancellation or lost or stolen luggage. Provided you pay for your ticket by credit card, you're usually covered for medical expenses and repatriation costs, but do check the extent of the cover offered with your credit card

company before leaving. If you make the bookings yourself, it's a good idea to take out cover for the cost of repatriation with an accredited insurance company.

USEFUL ADDRESSES

Tourism Flanders:
31 Pepper Street
London E14 9RW
☎ 020 7458 0044
(trade enquiries)
🖷 020 7458 0045
Public information line:
☎ 020 7867 0311
Brochure request line:
☎ 0891 887799 (60p per minute, provides detailed info covering northern Belgium including Brussels).
Email:
office@flanders-tourism.org

Belgian Tourist Board
(covers southern Belgium)
225 Marshall wall
London E14 9FW
☎ 020 7531 0392
🖷 020 7531 0393
Live operator:
☎ 0906 30 20 245
(50p per minute)
www.belgium-tourism.net
Email:
info@belgium-tourism.org

Belgian Embassy
103 Eaton Square
London SW1W 9AB
☎ 020 7470 3700
Visa information line:
☎ 0891 600 255

Belgian National Railways
Unit 200A
Blackfriars Boundary
156 Blackfriars Road
London SE1 8EN
☎ 020 7593 2332
🖷 020 7593 2333

HEALTH CARE

If you're following a course of medical treatment, ensure you take enough to cover the trip, as you can't be sure of finding it in Brussels. EU citizens are entitled to free medical treatment and medication (from doctors approved by the INAMI) on presentation of an E111 form, provided on request in advance of travel by your national sickness insurance provider. In the UK you can obtain an E111 from your post office.

CASH

The Belgian currency is the Belgian franc (BF), divided into 100 centimes. The notes come in denominations of BF100, 200, 500, 1000, 2000 and 10,000. The few coins in circulation are BF1, 5, 20, 50 and 50 centimes. Bureaux de change are located at the airport and in every station, but remember to change a little money before you leave, as there's no access to many of the automatic cash machines at the weekend. You can usually pay by credit card (Visa, Eurocard, Diner's Club, etc.) when you're shopping.

LOCAL TIME

Brussels is one hour ahead of Greenwich Mean Time, 6 hours ahead of the U.S.A and Canada (Eastern Standard Time), 8 hours behind Australia (East Coast) and 10 hours behind New Zealand.

VOLTAGE

In Belgium the current is 220 volts. Don't forget to take an adaptor with you, as Belgium has two-way plugs and sockets.

CHOCOLATE HEAVEN

Whether you're a reckless chocoholic or a gourmet who'll savour only the darkest bitter chocolate, make sure you try Belgian pralines. Inside the white, milk or dark chocolate shells the fillings of nuts, crèmes, liqueurs or simply more chocolate will melt in your mouth with amazing, unforgettable flavours. You'll have to decide for yourself which of the Brussels' chocolate makers is the best – just don't count the calories!

COCOA OR *CACAHUATL* ?

On their return from America the *conquistadores* brought back plants that were unknown in Europe, such as the potato, the tomato and cocoa. As they had no names for these plants, they also brought a few Aztec words to the Spanish court. 'Cocoa' is a phonetic transcription of the Nahuatl word *cacahuatl*, which comes from the Maya word *cacau*, whereas the Aztecs called their chocolate drink *xocatlatl*.

A DRINKABLE CURRENCY

Children who love to eat chocolate coins may be very surprised to know that the Maya and Aztecs paid for goods in cocoa beans. They also had the secret of a delicious drink, which was very nourishing according to the conquistador Hernan Cortez, who tasted it for the first time in 1519 at the court of the emperor

Montezuma. The Aztecs ground up grilled cocoa beans

and added either vanilla, cinnamon, nutmeg and honey or green maize, or fermented agave juice and pepper to make a luxury drink reserved exclusively for the nobility.

THE TASTE OF SIN

The Spanish improved the Aztec recipe by adding sugar, and soon none of them could do without their chocolate, even the monks and nuns. All the monasteries and convents in New Spain had a special place for making

chocolate. Questions were asked, however, as to whether these servants of God should really drink chocolate, as it was said to heat the blood and encourage the desires of the flesh. It's interesting to note, therefore, that it was the nuns of Puebla who invented the particular recipe of turkey with chocolate, known as *mole poblano*.

ELITIST SWEETNESS

It was Anne of Austria, daughter of Philip III of Spain, who brought cocoa beans home in her luggage in 1615, and introduced chocolate to the people of France. From there it made its way to England and in 1657 the first chocolate house opened in London. Chocolate as a beverage became the rage of the 17th-century London elite. From

London to Madrid, Paris to Brussels, it remained a luxury until the 19th century.

CHOCOLATE FOR ALL

In 1815 in Amsterdam, Kaspar van Houten discovered a process for separating part of the natural fat of the cocoa bean to produce cocoa butter and a more digestible product that could be reduced to powder. The chocolate industry was born, particularly since by this time cultivation of the cocoa plant had spread to Asia and Africa. Belgium's conquest of the Congo in 1885, under Leopold II, provided the Belgian chocolate industry

with new opportunities. In 1910 there were 73 chocolate manufacturers, whose production, strictly controlled by the state, established a reputation for fine quality.

PRALINES AND BALLOTINS

The praline, invented by confectioner Jean Neuhaus in 1921, is a small confection containing a nut or other sweet filling, covered in a thin chocolate coating. To stop them from being damaged by the traditional paper cone, Neuhaus invented a new type of packaging, a small cardboard box called a *ballotin*. Chocolate bars

of 30 and 45gm (10½ and 15¾ oz) were invented by Kwatta, also a Belgian. These bars, either plain or flavoured, are still one of manufacturer Côte d'Or's unrivalled specialities.

THE CHOCOLATE-MAKER'S SECRETS

The chocolate for coating is richer in fats but not as sweet as the finished product, and, processed into the form of liquid or drops, is used for making cakes and pralines. Two elements are vitally important if the final product is to have the right aroma and flavour: these are the origin of the beans (they can be either Criollo,

Trinitario or Forestaro), which are then combined in proportions kept secret by the manufacturer, and the way that they are ground.

PLANÈTE CHOCOLAT

24, Rue des Lombards
☎ **511 0755**
Tue.-Sat. 10am-6.30pm and Sun. 1-7pm.

If you'd like to nibble at a Grand-Place façade, a gothic church or some other work of art, just drop into Frank Duval's shop. He's a master chocolate-maker who produces his own pralines in the shop, pouring them into made-to-order moulds. Of course this great gourmet uses only ingredients of the finest quality in the creation of both his ephemeral works of art and in the hot chocolate you can sample in his beautiful café.

HOME OF COMICS

Cradle of the modern comic, homeland of Tintin, Spirou, Gaston Lagaffe, Fantasio, Alix and other heroes, Belgium celebrated a hundred years of the cartoon strip in 1997. The country produces 40 million comic books a year, of which 11 million are sold in Belgium. So why this fascination with cartoons, and how come this small country has the highest density of comic writers and illustrators per square mile in the whole world?

PICTURES THAT TALK

In a country where two languages and two cultures co-exist (not to mention the continual influx of invaders of various kinds, which lasted right up to the nineteenth century), visual language has had a deep impact on the population, who strive to communicate against all odds. In the 1950s Belgium was the country with the highest number of cinemas outside the USA. This attraction to the language of images and to the visual arts in general is no doubt one reason why Belgium has become the centre of the comic strip.

HERGÉ THE PIONEER

On 10 January 1929, the first adventure of a reporter called Tintin appeared in *Le Petit Vingtième*, the Thursday supplement of a Brussels' daily paper. It became so successful that in 1930 Hergé published the complete adventures of *Tintin in the Land of the Soviets* in the form of an album. The idea that a comic could be published as a book, with a proper hardback cover, and be kept on a shelf to be read and re-read, became one of the characteristics of Belgian comic production.

THE CULT OF THE HERO

Tintin is an empty and somewhat asexual character who can be placed in a wide range of settings. Though he was a colonialist in 1930, by 1975 he was siding with the guerillas. Characters in the newer comics often traded the role of the tough-guy hero for that of a more vulnerable, human figure with whom the reader could more easily identify.

THE SCHOOLS OF BRUSSELS AND MARCINELLE

By the 1950s Belgian comic production had polarised around two centres: Editions du Lombard in Brussels, with *Le Journal de Tintin* (*Tintin's Diary*) and the Dupuis company in Marcinelle, which launched the oldest comic in Belgium, the weekly *Spirou*, in 1938. Some have defined these two as schools, particularly the school of 'clear lines'

COMICS IN THE CITY

Horrified by the delapidated state of the houses in the city centre, comic strip illustrators got together to decorate whole walls. Ric Hochet, Victor Sackville, Lucky Luke, Boule et Bill and many other heroes can be seen as you wander around Brussels' streets. Don't miss *Le Passage* by Schuiten in Rue du Marché-au-Charbon (information about comic strip walks from the TIB ☎ 513 8940).

in Brussels. But in fact this simply reflects the impact of Hergé's powerful personality. He imposed a certain style on his collaborators, whereas the *Spirou* cartoonists around Jijé (Franquin, Peyo, Morris, Roba) were freer to establish their own different personal styles.

THE CLEAR LINE

The name 'clear line' appeared in the 1970s and is used to define a style invented by Hergé. In practice the type of drawing was a technical necessity due to poor production qualities of the *Petit Vingtième* newspaper. After the Second World War, this weekly supplement was replaced by *Le Journal de Tintin*, which was published in colour on better paper. This publication centred around Hergé, with future big names of the comic strip, including Jacobs, Martin, De Moor and Tibet.

SECOND WIND

When Tintin and Spirou's readers grew up they had nothing to read. However, 1959 saw the launch of the French magazine *Pilote,* headed by Goscinny. This at first targeted teenagers, but gradually evolved as its audience got older. This more mature audience for comics continued to grow and in 1978, in the Belgian town of Tournai, Casterman brought out the first issue of the monthly comic *À Suivre.* This featured work by both Belgian artists and the world's greatest comic strip authors, becoming a showcase for the diversity of contemporary comics.

THE COMIC CHARTS

'For young people from 7 to 77'. Today this slogan, coined by the *Tintin* magazine, is more relevant than ever,

since comics have grown up with their readers. There are now a wide range of titles with a huge readership. But though adult comics make up a major sector of the specialist magazine market, the titles with the widest circulation are still *Lucky Luke, Bob et Bobette* and *Asterix.*

THE COMIC MUSEUM (MUSÉE DE LA BANDE DESSINÉE)

20, Rue des Sables-1000
☎ 219 1980.
Open Tue.–Sun. 10am–6pm, closed 1 Jan. and 25 Dec. Access via stairs

from Boulevard Pacheco. Bus 38-Berlaimont.

By taking over the former Waucquez department store, an Art Nouveau gem designed by Horta in 1905, the museum saved the building, which was to be demolished to make way for a carpark. It was furiously defended by a group of comic fans and eventually became home to a museum devoted to comics. The displays are very educational, retracing the history of the comic strip with original plates: the Belgian pioneers from 1929 to 1960 and major trends from the 1960s to the present day, in Belgium and abroad. The exhibition of original plates is regularly changed for reasons of conservation.

SURREALISM THEN AND NOW

After spending a few hours in the European capital, you'll realise that it has a peculiar, slightly puzzling atmosphere. In this improbable city, created from a patchwork of nineteen districts full of contrast and contradictions, you never know when you'll come upon something weird and wonderful. It's not hard to understand why Brussels inspired Surrealist painters like Magritte and Delvaux.

André Breton

FROM PARIS TO BRUSSELS

1924, the year André Breton published the *Surrealist Manifesto* in Paris, also saw the birth of Surrealism in Brussels among a group of poets and artists. It grew out of their common feeling of 'rebellion against the world that is allotted to us and against the given, which is always humanly unacceptable'. It was primarily an ethical movement. When Magritte saw a reproduction of the *Song of Love* by the painter Giorgio de Chirico it was a revelation to him.

THE VISIONS OF MAGRITTE

Magritte came from the lower middle-class and shared his life with his wife Georgette and their Pomeranian dog. Uniquely, he would paint in his living-room in a suit and

bow tie. He was also a writer and poet, who never supplied any clues to understanding his art. His only message was that his pictures should be seen as a lesson and they should give the viewer a sense of mystery that makes them feel as if fantasy and reality were continually combining, an emotion he experienced throughout his childhood and youth. By continually playing with the processes of association and undermining our ideas of objects, he can place our own vision of the world in doubt.

NAKED WOMEN AND TRAINS

Paul Delvaux painted in a very different style to Magritte. Much maligned by him, Delvaux's work is more the fruit of his own natural outpourings, rather than of a desire to uncover a different kind of reality. His recurring landscapes, filled with temples, wandering

women, skeletons, trains and unanswered appeals, form an obsessional interior landscape. His images of anxiety (1938-1940) were followed by the strange paintings of a dreamer always filled with wonder.

A SURREALIST CAFÉ

La Fleur en Papier Doré was one of Magritte's favourite cafés. A framed photograph shows the owner, Geert Van Bruaene, with Magritte and his friends from the Society of Mystery, including the poets Elt Mesens, Louis Scutenaire, Paul Colinet and Camille Goemans. 'Long live Lautréamont' (a pre-Surrealist writer) is written on the wall in capital letters, along with aphorisms and pictures by the café owner, who was a fervent admirer and supporter of the Surrealists. The many kitsch objects were part of his dream concept, consisting of things whose uselessness made them poetic. (55, Rue des Alexiens-1000).

SURREALIST HALLUCINATIONS

Although Delvaux rarely visited the Art Nouveau café *Ultieme Hallucinatie*, its interior could have come straight out of one of his paintings. The wooden carriage seats in the winter garden, designed by Henry Van De Velde for the Belgian railway company SNCB, are arranged around tables and a caravan awning with a skylight. A ghostly female nude, which haunted Delvaux's nights, stands in the garden turned to stone. Sadly, the waterfalls which once graced the gardens of the Mont des Arts, where the Surrealists spent time engrossed in cryptic conversations, have been replaced by a cold acropolis. (*Ultieme Hallucinatie*: 316, Rue Royale-1210 ☎ 217 0614).

'FAÇADISM'

'Brusselisation' was followed by a new era, the age of 'façadism'. In this period the old buildings were still being destroyed, but a small part of their façades would be preserved. These would then be shored up and integrated into a modern construction, just like something painted by Magritte.

DECIPHERING THE CITY

The wide boulevards change their name depending on the side of the road you're on and the road leading to Mons is identical to the one leading to Bergen, for this is in fact the same city, Mons being the French name, Bergen the Flemish one – very confusing! Since 1989 Brussels has been the capital of Flemish-speaking Flanders, although 86% of the city's inhabitants speak French. The monumental law

courts have a dome 100m/330 ft high and a 3,600 m²/4,000 square yard waiting room. But it's the Gothic St Michel cathedral that takes the prize for Surrealism. Alongside it stands the church of the Flemish community, a futuristic building, bristling with steel tubes.

GIFT-WRAPPING THE BERLAYMONT BUILDING

Shock horror! In 1991 it was discovered that this four-pointed star of a building, erected in 1963 to house the European Commission, was full of asbestos. While waiting for a decision on whether this great European symbol should be demolished or decontaminated at enormous expense, the building has been wrapped in white cloth and, to make it more attractive, images are projected onto it at night.

ART NOUVEAU

By the early 20th century the population of Brussels had doubled and was suffocating inside its medieval walls. King Leopold II decided to bring some air into his capital by building suburbs and creating two wide, shady avenues, Avenue de Tervuren and Avenue de Louise. These became the favourite haunts of the financial and industrial bourgeoisie, who commissioned grand residences, designed by fashionable architects. These highly eclectic buildings are a true celebration of renewal.

ECONOMIC BOOM

The reign of Leopold II was a period of great prosperity. Belgian industry was expanding and the Congo, which the king had bought in 1885, was a source of enormous riches, including precious woods and ivory. The new middle classes were liberal, enlightened and progressive. They turned their backs on the old values, asserting their independence and the originality of their new ideas by encouraging a wide range of experimentation in architecture, mainly

featuring new materials such as iron and glass.

PERSONALISED HOUSES

Art Nouveau was seen as a liberating revolution against the tedious similarity of the old 19th-century façades which, even when they were intended to be ostentatious, turned out to be depressingly monotonous. Paul Hankar was one of the first to reject this mediocrity by designing houses that were all different,

with wide doors and windows topped with colourful arches. Another major figure, Victor Horta, abandoned the plan of three interconnecting rooms, which still characterises many houses in Brussels, bringing light into the heart of the home.

A MARRIAGE OF TECHNICAL SKILL AND IMAGINATION

In the 19th century, Japan was reopened to the outside world and the influence of its sober, pared-down art spread far and wide. This, combined with the new industrial technologies and the import of marble and precious woods from the Congo, stimulated the architects experimenting with designs for flexible, modern housing that was adapted to the needs of its inhabitants. Free of the old constraints they turned to plants and Gothic designs for inspiration.

A HOUSE-CUM-MANIFESTO

With its narrow façade galvanised by an all-glass bow window, the massive, overt use of iron with its rivets clearly visible, and its yellow and blue

stonework, the Hotel Tassel, built by Victor Horta in 1893, remains a key building in the history of architecture. In particular it's the way that the rooms inside are laid out around a superb spiral staircase and the decoration – including the famous 'whiplash' – that reveal the genius of the man who was to become the uncontested leader of the Art Nouveau movement.

LUXURY AND SENSUALITY

With the support of his industrialist friends, Horta was given an entirely free rein to design Art Nouveau's most striking buildings, of which the Hotel Solvay is the finest and most luxurious. Horta considered every single detail: he chose all the materials himself, from mahogany from the Congo to padauk from Burma, and designed everything down to the smallest elements of the decor, from the radiators to the door handles. It goes without saying

ART AND INDUSTRY

Philippe Denys Antiques, 1, Rue des Sablons-1000
☎ 512 3607
Open Tue.–Sat. 10.30am–1pm, 2–6.30pm, Sun. 10.30am–1.30pm.

Art Nouveau was undoubtedly an elitist art. Gustave Serrurier, a cabinet maker from Liège, wanted to mass-produce his furniture. Although he managed to set up a business employing around a hundred workers, he didn't make a lot of money, as potential customers demanded unique items. Today Serrurier-Bovy furniture is becoming increasingly popular and collectors rush to the few antique dealers who stock it.

that the wallpaper, carpets and furniture are all unique and were specially designed to suit each room.

TOWARDS MODERNISM

Henry Van de Velde, who started out as a painter, was utterly opposed to the extravagant fantasy and proliferation of decoration to which Horta's followers were too often prone. Rigour, minimalism and purity of line were his watchwords, making him a forerunner of the design movement. After a stay in

Germany, where he headed the school that would become the famous Bauhaus, in 1926 he opened La Cambre Institute of Decorative Arts, which is still open today and very highly regarded.

PALAIS STOCLET

Built between 1905 and 1911 by Viennese architect Josef Hoffmann, this building marks the end of the period of exuberance and fantasy. Its refined façade, pronounced straight lines, covered with marble and discreet bronze decoration, reflects the movement towards Art Deco. Unfortunately the interior, decorated by Klimt, is not open to the public. (271-281, Av. de Tervuren).

THE BRUSSELS' SPIRIT

The experience of sharing their city between two peoples, the Walloons and the Flemish, and coping with the presence of Spanish, Austrian, French and Dutch invaders has given the citizens of Brussels a mistrust of words and principles, the capacity to ignore authority and a wonderful sense of humour, called *zwanze*, which enables them to laugh at anything, including themselves.

THE FIRST ZWANZER

At the height of the Spanish occupation, it was Brueghel the Elder, an inhabitant of Marolles, who first practised the art of *zwanze* in his painting. At first sight *The Massacre of the Innocents* is just another biblical scene, but it's set in a village on the outskirts of Brussels and Herod's soldiers are wearing the despised uniform of the Duke of Alba. Besides criticising Spanish violence, he also portrayed everyday life with sympathy and humour – look as long as you like, you'll never find the husband among the excited revellers in *The Wedding Feast*.

WOLTJE AND MANNEKENPIS

A puppet that tells *flauwskes* (silly jokes) every evening at the Théâtre de Toone, and the statue of a little boy doing a pee on a street corner, are the true heroes of Brussels. They are far more famous than Dukes d'Egmont and de Hornes, who led an uprising against Philip II of Spain and were beheaded on the Grand-Place, although

Mannekenpis *did* sprinkle water on a bomb which threatened to blow up the city hall! King Louis XV of France was not without wit and gave the statue an embroidered coat to ask forgiveness for the bad behaviour of his soldiers, who had stolen the statue in 1747.

A CITY WITHOUT PERSPECTIVES

Search all you like, but you won't find a single perspective view in Brussels. The Royal Palace is approached from the side; the great thoroughfare of the Rue de la Loi turns its back on the arch of the Cinquantenaire; what you see at the end of the famous Avenue de Tervueren is not the famous Congo Museum but a private house; the

Saint-Michel cathedral is wedged between tall, modern apartment blocks and the view of Grand-Place is hidden by a series of hotels built in a reproduction 'old' style. Brussels has deliberately decided not to show off its monuments to good effect. It's up to you to try and find the best angle for a photograph!

OUT AND ABOUT IN MAROLLES

Round, jolly faces, toothless or ironic grins, beer drinkers leaning on the bar or sleeping at an alehouse table – here you'll find all the rogues and beggars captured by Brueghel. Not long ago you could still witness some truly burlesque

scenes, such as closing time at *Le Bossu*, when the owner would untie the rope stretched across the room over which her drunken clients had collapsed. If you'd like to get a flavour of the local *brusseleir* dialect, drop into *Chez Alex* or *Le Coq*, the last authentic cafés in Marolles, and listen to the very vocal elderly locals. It's the best way to get an idea of their very particular kind of humour, and even if you can't

understand a word they're saying, you can still soak up the atmosphere and a beer.

BRUSSELEIR

The real Brussels' *zinneke* ('bastard') is the only Belgian for whom the quarrel between Flemish and French simply does not exist. Living in a city hated by the Flemish, who don't feel at home here, and rejected by the French-speaking Walloons for supporting the Jacobins in the French Revolution, a *zinneke* speaks a colourful dialect, a mixture of Flemish and French, with words taken from the languages of the various occupiers, such as *moukère* (*mujer*) meaning 'woman'.

THE CAFÉ

With its polished wood and gleaming pumps, this is the quintessential meeting place. It's here that Belgians come to imbibe a good proportion of the 264 pints/120 litres of beer they each drink on average in a year. But remember: the way the beer is served is a very serious matter. Each type has a corresponding glass of the best possible size and shape, a correct temperature and a way of pouring that doesn't shake up the yeast deposit at the bottom of the bottle. And if the owner wants a boring customer to leave, he simply places a metal figurine, known as a *zageman*, on his table.

TINTIN AMONG THE BELGIANS

There's always an element of Hergé's humour that just can't be explained to Tintin's non-Belgian readers. Did you know that in reality the Picaros and the Arumbayas spoke the same language? That King Ottokar IV's motto is *'Eih Bennek, Eih Blavek'* ('I'm here, I'm staying' in the Brussels dialect) and that Colonel Spons is Colonel Sponge? French speakers could always try reading Tintin with the *Dictionnaire du dialecte bruxellois*. (Louis Quiévreux).

BRUSSEL
BRUXELLES
GRAND PLACE / TAPIS DE FLEURS
GROTE MARKT, BLOEMENTAPIJT

LAMBIC AND GUEUSE, THE LOCAL BREW

Of the 400-or-so varieties of Belgian beer, there is one whose flavour cannot be that different from the brew drunk by the Ancient Egyptians and Sumerians 5,000 years ago. Gueuse beer is a drink halfway between wine and beer, obtained through spontaneous fermentation. A long process of ageing in the cask gives it a depth and subtlety that completely disproves the myth that beer is a drink lacking in refinement. Gueuse is the pride of Brussels and they say that it can be brewed only in the area between Halle and Vilvorde. It is the last beer still to be brewed using a process of spontaneous fermentation following Pasteur's discovery of the secret of yeast in the 19th century.

STAGE ONE: BREWING

The grains of wheat (35%) and malted barley (65%) are first

crushed before being poured into a vat of water heated to a temperature of 72°C. After two hours the saccharification process converting the starch into sugar is complete and the wort (a sweet deposit of malt and wheat left at the bottom of the vat) is pumped into large boiling vats containing turning blades. At this point hops (at least three years old to avoid any excessive bitterness) are added in greater quantities

than in other beers. This facilitates the preservation of the beer and gives it its flavour. The beer is boiled for three hours and loses about a quarter of its total volume through evaporation, but this raises its sugar content, and therefore its alcohol content.

FERMENTATION FROM NATURAL CULTURE

The liquid is then pumped into large, shallow basins placed in the well-ventilated roof space of the brewery, where it cools over night, passing from a

temperature of 95° to 20°C (203 to 68°F). This is the magic moment when the culture forms spontaneously, brought about by naturally occurring ferments, including *Brettanomyces bruxellensis,* which is present in the air of the Senne valley. It is these ferments that give gueuse its unique taste. Now all that remains is to move the precious liquid into oak or chestnut pipes (650 litres/178 gallons) or barrels (250 litres/69 gallons).

THE *LAMBIC* EMERGES

After a few days a spontaneous process of fermentation begins, in which the wort is transformed into alcohol and CO_2. For the first four weeks this is so rapid that the barrels cannot be closed due to the risk that they might explode. Fermentation gradually slows down and becomes more complex over a three-year period, producing a flat beer with an acidic taste and subtle flavours that develop in your mouth. This drink is known as *lambic*. It can be drunk in its pure form at the brewery or in very few cafés in Brussels (*La Bécasse*) which sell it in sufficient quantities, as it starts to lose its quality once the barrel is opened. You can also buy a variety known as *faro*, consisting of *lambic* with added cane sugar.

GUEUSE, THE CHAMPAGNE OF BEERS

To obtain gueuse beer, the master brewer selects five or six *lambics* which are one, two and three years old. The younger ones provide the natural sugars necessary for further fermentation, while the older ones give the beer its refined smell and taste. After fermenting further in the bottle over several months, the gueuse becomes sparkling and

acidic, with a flavour not unlike cider. The taste varies from year to year and according to the blend. The most unusual versions are those where fruit is added to the beer. Morello cherries picked in late summer are soaked in a two-year-old *lambic* for three months before it is bottled. The slightly acidic beer that results is called Kriek.

This is a real delight, very refreshing and with an almond aftertaste. The heady, sparkling and strongly flavoured raspberry beer is the pink champagne of beers.

A LIVING MUSEUM: BRASSERIE CANTILLON

56, Rue Gheude-1070 (Bus 47-Liverpool)
☎ 521 4928
Open Mon.–Fri. 8.30am–5pm, Sat. 10am–5pm, Entry charge.

Of the dozens of breweries that have plied their trade in Brussels since the sixteenth century, only two small producers, one of which is the Cantillon family, have avoided takeover by the big national groups. Making real gueuse beer takes a lot of time and money. It can be brewed only in the cold season, from October to April, and only about 15 *brassins* or 900 hectolitres/250 gallons a year are made. But the finished product is totally different from Bellevue's industrial gueuse. If you're in Brussels during the cold season make sure you go on a tour of the Cantillon brewery. You may be lucky enough to be present at a morning's brewing and in any case you'll get an opportunity to taste the product.

BRUSSELS IN BLOOM

With its 4,000 hectares/ 10,000 acres of parks and woodland, amounting to a quarter of its entire area, Brussels is second only to Washington, USA, in the list of the world's greenest cities, with 40 m²/48 sq yards of grass for each inhabitant, leaving aside the many private houses that have gardens. As you wander through their parks and gardens you'll realise that people in Brussels tend not to be great fans of brick and concrete, instead they are people with a true passion for nature.

BRUSSELS IN FLOWER

The flower season opens in April in the old botanic gardens, where you can gaze at the magnificent beds planted with 2,500 irises of 40 different varieties. In May the royal greenhouses of Laeken are open to the public for two weeks. As well as the great beauty of A. Balat's city of glass and iron (1887), which houses a tropical forest of giant palms, coconut trees and tree ferns, visitors are amazed by the riotous colours of the azaleas, hortensias and

fuchsias carpeting its glass-lined avenues. Meanwhile on the weekend of 15 August

(every evenly numbered year) Grand-Place is entirely covered in a wonderful carpet of begonias.

FROM PARK TO PARK

The Parc Royal in the very centre of the city, with its geometrical design dotted with mythological statues, the unexpected Egmont park,

GOOD TO KNOW

**The Royal greenhouses in Laeken
Entrance at the corner of Av. du Parc-Royal and Av. Van Praet
Bus 53-Gros Tilleul
Info: ☎ 504 0390 or 513 8940.
Musée David et Alice Van Buuren
41, Av. Léo Errera-1180
☎ 343 4851.**

Garden tours every day, 2–6pm. Entry charge.

hidden behind the Hilton hotel, and the great park of Cinquantenaire are all havens of peace, much appreciated by the citizens of Brussels. Yet there are other parks that are just as attractive, some of which even the locals don't really know about. Tervuren, with its large lakes and an arboretum, is the most popular destination for a Sunday walk. Tournay-Solvay park in Boitsfort, with its romantic, neo-Renaissance ruined

château, has a fine rose garden, while vast Duden park (23 hectares/57 acres) in Forest is a wild wood. Lastly, Josaphat park in Schaerbeek is planted with rare species such as the Virginia tulip tree and is decorated with rockeries and ornamental lakes.

AN ART DECO GARDEN IN UCCLE

Like most of the inhabitants of Brussels, the Van Buurens, who were collectors and patrons of the arts, couldn't imagine having a house without a garden. Their own garden stretches for more than a hectare/2½ acres behind their Art Deco house and was designed as an extension of their home. Like the building's bay windows and the furniture inside it, the hundred-year-old maples, wild lemon trees and mineral

elements in this picturesque garden, which was designed by J. Buyssens, reflect a

Japanese influence. You can also lose yourself wandering through the maze of 300 yew trees that leads to the seven leafy chambers illustrating the *Song of Songs*.

SEMI-WILD PLACES

Fifteen minutes from the city centre, between Molenbeek and Jette, a series of inter-connecting, swampy open spaces have been miraculously preserved within this urban area. You can cycle or walk through the 126 ha/310 acres, ranging from vegetable plots to meadows, woods and marshland full of frogs, herons and kingfishers, where you're also quite likely to spot a fox or two.

THE FOREST OF SOIGNES

This vast forest, with its magnificent, towering beeches two hundred years old, stretches for 4,380 ha/10,800 acres to the south of the city. Its grassy hollows, ruined abbeys such as Rouge-Cloître and many lakes have all provided inspiration for painters and poets. La Cambre wood on the edge of the forest, created in 1862 to plans by the German designer E. Keilig, is a particularly fine example of landscaping. La Cambre abbey with its 14th-century church, 16th-century cloister and tiered gardens is one of the most attractive places in the city.

SECRET GARDEN

49, Rue du Magistrat, 1050
☎ **649 3949**
Tue.–Sat., 11am–7pm.

In his little mossy grotto, where water burbles in a stone basin, Thierry Boutemy, from Honfleur in France, creates works of ephemeral beauty. He lovingly produces wonderful compositions using wild flowers, which he buys every morning from the small market gardens around Brussels. Primary colours and subtle, woody scents mingle in these little bouquets, which will fill your home with their lasting perfume.

KING OF THE BELGIANS

In 1830 Belgium became independent, but had neither a constitution nor a head of state. After several months of debate, the European powers organised the election of a National Congress, which chose a prince of the Saxe-Cobourg-Gotha family as king. Leopold I swore his coronation oath on 21 July 1831. So who are this royal family, who never make the headlines and whose pictures seldom appear in either the tabloid papers or the popular magazines?

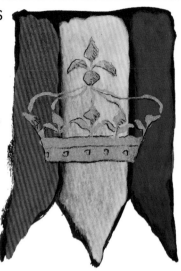

CHRONICLE OF A ROYAL DEATH

The sudden death of King Baudouin in 1993 plunged the whole of Belgium into mourning. For two days nearly 50,000 people filed past as his body lay in state. The Belgians were caught between sorrow and confusion, which was a surprisingly excessive reaction when you think that there had been absolutely no visible trace of royal influence on Belgian politics throughout the king's 42-year reign. He was such a discreet monarch that they'd almost forgotten his existence.

ORPHAN BELGIUM

Deprived of any executive power when his father Leopold III abdicated following the Royal Question, Baudouin, who was crowned on 17 July 1951, was condemned to become a shadowy figure, whose only power was over the appointment of the Prime Minister. The slow fragmentation of his kingdom, which became a federal state in 1992, gave him a dual role of mediation and conciliation. 'The cement of Belgium', 'Father of the Nation' cried the press the day after his death, as though the very survival of Belgium depended on him.

ALBERT AND PAOLA

Everyone was expecting the king's nephew Philippe to be crowned. He had been preparing to take over from his aging uncle for years. But in the end it was his father, Baudouin's brother, Albert, who became the 6th king of the Belgians. After a great many consultations Baudouin's wife, Queen Fabiola, stayed on at Laeken Palace, while Albert and Paola reign from the Belvédère. The storm has passed and the palace has returned to its routine, with one major difference: unlike Fabiola, Paola loves fashion and at last she has the chance to put this to good use as an ambassador for Belgian fashion designers.

CHÂTEAU LIFE

No changing of the guard, no fashionable receptions, no grand balls, no processions or waving from carriages, and above all no scandals. Unlike their British cousins, the Belgian monarchs keep themselves very much to themselves, with none of the trappings of royalty. If Louise and Stéphanie, the daughters of Leopold II are to be believed, château life was anything but fun, even if their father was – rightly – thought to have had a few amorous adventures. It was only after the death of his wife Marie-Henriette that he introduced his mistress, a young French woman called Blanche Delacroix, known as 'Baronne de Vaughan', who gave him two sons, Lucien and Philippe.

A HEREDITARY PASSION FOR BEAUTIFUL CARS

A VERY BELGIAN COMPROMISE

King Baudouin, a devout Catholic and husband of the equally devout Fabiola, faced a terrible crisis of conscience when the Prime Minister asked him to sign a new law decriminalising abortion. He felt unable to continue on the throne and, on 4 April 1990, he abdicated ... for 36 hours, just long enough for ministers to set their own signatures to the offending text.

Leopold II was the first of the royal family to be an interested visitor to the Paris Motor Show. He owned several powerful Mercedes, which he tended to drive rather fast. Since his day the press have continually referred to the royal passion for expensive cars. Apparently, Baudouin used to drive his car up and down the avenues in the grounds at Laeken, never daring to pass through the gates. His brother Albert has always been more interested in motorbikes.

AN ELIGIBLE BATCHELOR

It's not easy to find a fiancée when you are the heir to the throne. You can't marry without the approval of the king and queen, on pain of losing your right to succession. In the case of the Belgian royal family, the 'right' wife must fulfil moral and

linguistic conditions (be a practising Catholic and speak the two national languages), be excellently educated and – of course – of noble blood. Perhaps the fact that the timid Philippe, born in 1960, was still unmarried may have contributed to him not succeeding to the throne. Particularly as his sister, Astrid, who married Archduke Lorenz d'Autriche-Este, can now claim succession following the recent modification of an article of the constitution.

King Leopold II

UNDERGROUND ART

Having buried its museum of modern art, Brussels now also puts contemporary works on show in the Metro. Perhaps the city can find no place on the surface for 20th- and 21st-century artistic expression, or perhaps modern art is easier to understand when you're a few feet under the ground.

A MUSEUM IN THE BASEMENT

Following an argument between the preservers of the architectural heritage and those who advocated building

a modern art museum near Place Royale, it was decided to build the museum underground. A 65,000m³/ 85,000cu. yd hole contains seven floors of galleries, arranged in a semicircle around a well of light. This very beautiful building by the Belgian architect Roger Bastin was opened in 1984.

MODERN ART ON THE WALLS

When does modern art begin and end? Although the museum's collections don't

contain many works by foreign artists, they do give a good representation of Belgian painting and sculpture from the end of the 19th century to 1940. The 19th-century artists include James Ensor, Navez, Stevens, De Braekeleer and Van Rysselberghe. The fauvist colours of Rik Wauters, Spilliaert's maritime reveries, the mystical images of Laethem-Saint-Martin and the Flemish expressionists occupy

a large part of the early 20th-century galleries. Major works by Magritte and a few by Delvaux reflect aspects of Surrealism in Belgium. Works by Victor Servranckx, a forerunner of abstract art, who began painting non-figurative works in 1917, are also shown.

THE COBRA GROUP

The short-lived Cobra movement, named after the home cities of its artist members (**Co**penhagen, **Br**ussels, **A**msterdam), was the last manifestation of northern expressionism and gave rise to one of the liveliest currents in post-war art. The Cobra artists advocated spontaneous gestures and drew on different influences including untrained and 'primitive' art, cinema and writing. Dotremont, who co-founded the movement in 1948,

advocated non-specialisation and experimented with 'word-paintings' with Alechinsky. (Metro Anneessens.)

ABSTRACT ART

Jo Delahaut and Pol Bury, co-authors of the *Manifesto*

of *Spatialism* in 1954, had different approaches to art: Delahaut experimented with colour in a minimalist style while Bury explored the possibilities of optical and kinetic art, rejecting any expression of feeling. (Metro Montgoméry or Metro Bourse.)

AFTER 1958

This can be seen as the point where contemporary art begins, the kind you can sometimes see in museums, but more often are in private galleries. In the absence of any real policy for buying works by active artists, the city of Brussels has taken the praiseworthy step of asking some well-established and highly respected Belgian artists to provide decorations for the metro, which opened in 1976.

ART IN THE METRO

Hyperrealism, Constructivism, action painting, neo-figuratives, neo-Fauvists... there are as many terms as there are artists. The best way to find out about them is to see their work by taking a trip on the metro. From station to station for BF50, the price of a metro ticket, you can explore the work of the painters and sculptors who have used the environment (speed, underground world) to make works that have a synergy with the space around them.

ART TICKET

Start your trip at Montgoméry, where **Folon**'s *Magic City* offeres a menacing vision of the future, while **Pol Mara** shows stereotyped images from our own time in six panels. The ceramics on the wall are by **Jo Delahaut**. On line 1A, at Thiéffry station, you can see **Félix Roulin**'s human bodies trying to free themselves from a flow of molten bronze. Continue on line 1 to Botanique to admire *The last Migration*, a monumental flight of the imagination by sculptor **Jean-Pierre Ghysels**, and the twelve multicoloured travellers by **Pierre Caille**. Then take the pre-metro to Bourse, where **Delvaux**'s images of old trams contrast with the slow movements of **Pol Bury**'s steel cylinders. Continue for one more station, and you can complete your tour with an exploration of *Les Sept Écritures*, the beautiful 'logogrammes' by **Dotremont** and **Alechinsky.** at Anneessens.

Ne pas plier s.v.p./Niet plooien a.u.b.

I VOYAGE
I RIT

STIB
MIVB

CT197

A oblitérer à chaque entrée en station ou, en surface, dans chaque véhicule.
A conserver jusqu'à la sortie de la station ou, en surface, jusqu'à la descente du véhicule.
Utilisable trois ans à dater de l'achat.
Autres conditions de validité: voir tarifs en vigueur.

Afstempelen telkens man een station be-treedt of bovengronds een voertuig instapt Moet bewaard worden tot het station of bovengronds het voertuig verlaten wordt.
Bruikbaar tot drie jaar na aankoop.
Andere geldigheidsvoorwaarde: Zo geldend tariat.

BEHIND THE SCENES IN EUROPE'S CAPITAL

As a market town founded over a thousand years ago on the route from Bavai to Cologne, now the capital of a young state riven by quarrels over language, what future would there have been for Brussels without the signing of the Treaty of Rome in 1957? Brussels gave itself to Europe because it couldn't carry on by itself, isolated as it was between Wallonia and Flanders. But there was another side to the coin: Europe brought with it inflated housing costs, depopulation, congested roads and deep wounds in the city's already mistreated urban fabric. This explains the lack of interest – and indeed rejection – felt by the people of Brussels for the European institutions.

STRASBOURG OR BRUSSELS?

Much is at stake in the rivalry between the two cities, as the economic effects of the presence of the European institutions and the activities associated with them bring in about 65 billion francs a year to Brussels. This is one major reason why Strasbourg is not about to give up its Euro MPs. However, Brussels has recently built all the necessary infrastructure. Apart from the old Berlaymont building, currently under renovation due to the presence of asbestos, 1995 saw the opening of the Council of Europe, an enormous granite bunker covering 200,000m^2/50 acres, followed more recently by the enormous, new CIC

conference centre, a 600,000m^2/60 acre building designed to house the new semicircular Parliament... but only for supplementary sessions!

UNPOPULAR CIVIL SERVANTS

No matter how many times the people of Brussels are told that the presence of the European Commission is a blessing, the fact remains that they find the

lifestyles of the European civil servants extremely irritating. Their very large salaries, supplemented by a great many privileges such as accommodation allowances, relocation expenses, tax immunity and exclusive access to duty-free shops, are all sources of resentment for the ordinary citizens, who pay very heavy taxes out of their very modest salaries. This has created a divide between the population and the Eurocrats, who show a certain disdain for their hosts, but are nevertheless greatly appreciated by the city's restaurant-owners, hoteliers and shopkeepers.

BRUSSELS COMMITS HARI-KIRI

The arrival of the European institutions dealt the death-blow to a city that had already been gutted. The Léopold district, much-favoured by the bourgeoisie around 1850, was flattened by the bulldozers. Its beautiful residences gave way to huge, hideous postmodern towers, thrown up in a hurry, with no overall plan and linked after the event with walkways. A real treasure-hunt for newly arrived Eurocrats trying to find their meeting in *Breydel, Charlemagne, Juste Lipse* or the *Caprice des Dieux*. Yet the Résidence Palace, an Art Deco jewel dating from 1926, owes its survival to these same Eurocrats , who are the only ones now allowed to dive into its magnificent swimming pool. .

SPEED IS THE PRIORITY

Since 1835, when Brussels opened the first railway in Europe, Belgium's politicians have wanted to make the city into the continent's centre. In 1900 entire neighbourhoods were flattened to create the major junction between the Gare du Nord and the Gare du Midi, which are 2km/1 mile apart. The work was started under Leopold II and the junction was opened under Baudouin 50 years later in 1952. The stations are currently undergoing their third facelift to accommodate the high-speed TGV trains. The city's ringroads and high speed routes should make Brussels easier to get to, but when you get to the end of the motorway there are no road signs to tell the lost traveller how to get to the city centre.

AN URBAN PLANNER'S DREAM

Among architects the term 'Brusselisation' is synonymous with the destruction of the urban fabric, an implicit criticism of the attitude of the Belgian politicians who destroy the old to make way for the new. Sadly they are spoilt for choice when it comes to awarding the annual 'golden bulldozer' award to the most

effective destroyer of the country's heritage. No surprise then that the term *archietek* has become a bit of an insult.

LITTLE MANHATTAN

In the late 1960s Vanden Boynants, head of the department of public works, and the property developer Charly de Pauw dreamed of transforming Brussels into a little Manhattan. On the

pretext that the city needed a new European dimension, 53ha/130 acres behind the Gare du Nord were flattened to build the World Trade Centre. Twenty-five years later this profitable operation consists of four towers randomly spaced among the cranes on a vast empty space 1km/½ mile from Grand-Place. There aren't even any offices for the Eurocrats.

DELVAUX, A LOVE OF LEATHER

There are two companies that still grant themselves the luxury of producing leather items entirely by hand – Hermès in Paris and Delvaux in Brussels. Buying a Delvaux bag is an expensive purchase, but it's also a gift to yourself that you can keep for the rest of your life without worrying that it'll ever go out of fashion. In fact the *Brillant* model, designed for Expo '58, is still the famous brand's best-selling bag.

FROM LUGGAGE TO HANDBAGS

The company, founded by Charles Delvaux in 1829, targeted its products at wealthy customers who needed solid leather luggage and high-quality travel items for their long transatlantic crossings, chaotic journeys in Pullman carriages and trips to spas. In 1933 the business was bought by Franz Schwennicke, who steered it in the direction of its current production of luxury leather goods to accompany designer clothing.

A COLLECTION IS BORN

Six months! That's how long it takes for a new design to come into being, from the first sketch to the creation of the prototype. When the designer has finished drawing the piece, a first version is made up and any technical adjustments and refinements made. It takes three months to make one of these models using 'salpa', a mixture of cardboard and leather onto which the tooling is drawn.

A HIGHLY SPECIALISED CRAFT

Whether they're paring down the leather in preparation for sewing or folding, threading the edges using Indian ink and paraffin or sewing together pieces that have already been glued, the exceptional quality of finish is determined by the skill of the craftspeople who work on it. It takes two years to train machinists, after which they are able to tool the leather without visible joins and can guide the needle on the machine to create the famous saddle stitch.

CALF OR OSTRICH?

High-quality skin is obviously of prime importance. Calf skin and the skins of farmed ostriches and crocodiles are the most highly prized, with a clear preference for smooth or grainy calf. Ostrich skin with its characteristic texture (each bead marks the place where a feather has been plucked) acquires a lovely sheen as it ages, unlike crocodile skin, which dulls. This characteristic, added to the fact that the process of treating the skin on the flesh side takes a very long time, explains why ostrich skin is so expensive. An ostrich skin bag is three or four times as much as a calf skin one.

A JUSTIFIED PRICE

When you realise that a piped bag is first designed entirely inside-out and then turned and lined with lambskin, that it takes fifteen return trips from the glueing table to the machinist to put a bag together, and that it takes between six and thirteen hours' work to make each bag, it puts the price of this luxury item into its proper perspective.

EXTREMELY EXCLUSIVE

Apart from very particular shades such as *rosso* (bordeaux), *ravello* (rich

HOW TO LOOK AFTER YOUR BAG

Don't leave leather out in the sun, wipe away any splashes of water immediately, treat greasy stains using talcum powder after you have removed any excess grease with paper tissue and regularly moisturise your leather bag with an appropriate cream.
For more serious accidents Delvaux has now opened a restoration service, which can perform small miracles.

brown), daffodil yellow or airforce blue (blue-grey), Delvaux also invented *toile de cuir* or 'leather cloth'. This is a weave of fine strips of leather on a polyamide chain. Infinite variations are possible by altering the thickness and colour of the weave.

BY APPOINTMENT TO THE COURT

Since being awarded the quality mark of Court supplier in 1883, Delvaux has had a specially favoured relationship with the Gotha family. Paola carried her first crocodile bag, a gift from Delvaux, at the time of her engagement to Prince Albert in 1959. Its role on this occasion gave the bag the name 'great happiness' and it is still one of the classic bags today. When Paola became queen she remained a faithful Delvaux client.

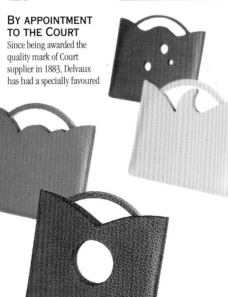

Brussels Practicalities

GETTING AROUND

Most tourists spend about 3 hours on their visit to Brussels and assume that the city consists entirely of the Grand-Place and a mussels-and-chips restaurant, but it's important to realise that if you want to get a good idea of what Brussels is like beyond the area of its central pentagon, you'll need at least two days. Don't waste your time trying to drive around the centre – there are hardly any parking places and the police are particularly quick to pack your car off to the pound, whether it's blocking the traffic or not. It's much better to park in one of the free zones (near the Sainte-Catherine metro station, for example). You can easily walk round the centre, as the main points of interest are fairly close to each other. But if you want to follow the 'Art Nouveau' or 'Cinquantenaire' itineraries, buy an STIB card at the nearest metro station as soon as you arrive. You can use this on any form of public transport. If you've come to Brussels by car, it's more practical to use it in the evening and on Sundays, when public transport services are less frequent, and especially to visit suburban areas, where it's much easier to park. If you do this, make sure you take a detailed map of the city as there aren't many road signs and those there are tend to be highly unreliable.

BY METRO, TRAM AND BUS

Public transport in Brussels runs from 5am to midnight. The city centre is well served by the underground railway, known as the metro, (2 lines) and by trams that run in tunnels (which are known as *prémétros*). To get to areas outside the central pentagon, you'll often have a choice of either tram (rather slow) or bus. You can get a detailed plan of the city in any metro station.

You can buy individual tickets (BF50) in the metro and from bus or tram drivers. If you expect to use public transport more frequently, it's better to buy a day pass (BF130) or a pass for 5 (BF240) or 10 journeys (BF320). These magnetic cards have to be validated in ticket-punching machines each time you use the bus, tram or metro. They're valid for one hour and you can use them on any combination of public transport (STIB, DE LIJN and TEC). You can buy them in metro stations (from machines), at STIB kiosks (Rogier, Porte de Namur, Gare du Midi and Bourse) or in newsagents.

BY TAXI

Taxis offer a handy way to get to your hotel from the airport or station, though taxis are on the expensive side here (BF95 minimum charge plus BF38 per km in central Brussels and the city's 19 districts, double that outside Brussels itself). On the other hand, there's no extra charge for luggage and prices don't increase at night. Expect to pay about BF1,000 from the airport and BF200-300 for a journey within Brussels. From the airport, you're best off with an *Autolux* taxi (☎ 411 4142), which will give you a 20 % discount if you use the same company for your return journey. Once in the city, it's best to call a cab by phone as taxi ranks are rare.

Green taxis ☎ 349 4949.
Blue taxis ☎ 268 0000.
Taxi Hendriks ☎ 752 9800 (equipped to carry disabled people, book 2–3 days in advance).

PARKING

Make sure you have plenty of BF5 and 20 coins to put in parking meters (BF25 for one hour). Parking is free on Sundays and from 1.30–2.30pm on weekdays. Remember that car park buildings (BF55 for one hour) are closed at night from 1-6.30am.

Fourrière Radar
47-51, Rue du Vieux-Marché-aux-Grains-1000
☎ 502 5050.

USING THE TELEPHONE

To make a call to a number outside Belgium,

dial 00 followed by the dialling code for the country you're ringing and the usual area code and individual number of the person you're ringing, leaving off the first zero of their number.

To call a Brussels number simply dial the 7-figure number, preceded by 02 if you're calling from somewhere else in Belgium.

There are comparatively few public telephones and they're all different. Most of them take phone cards (BF200, 500 or 1000), which can be bought in post offices, newsagents and the stores known as 'night shops'.

The others take BF5 and 20 coins (BF10 minimum). Off-peak rates for international calls apply on Sundays and 8pm-8am the rest of the week.

PHONE CARDS

You can buy these in 'night shops', bureaux de change and newsagents. They enable you to call from

any telephone, including private numbers or your hotel. You dial the number on the card, followed by the number you want to call. You'll be told the amount left on your card at the start of each call. These cards come in values of BF200, 500 and 1000 and give you calls at a rate 20% cheaper than that of Belgacom.
Lastly, if you ring from your hotel room remember that you'll have to pay a hefty surcharge on top of the price of the call.

USING THE POST

You can buy stamps in any post office. These are open from 9am–6pm Monday to Friday. The post office at the Gare du Midi is open 24 hours, the one in the Centre Monnaie (Bd Anspach) is open till 7pm on weekdays and from 10am–3pm on Saturdays. The price of a stamp for a 20gm/7oz letter is BF19. Letterboxes are red.

THE ATOMIUM

The Atomium is outside the centre of Brussels, but you must go and see it. It's a large iron molecule, 165 billion times bigger than life-size, whose nine spheres host different exhibitions all year round. In a couple of minutes you'll be shot up to the top of the Atomium, from where you'll have a magnificent view over Brussels and the Brabant area. Metro: Heysel/Heizel.

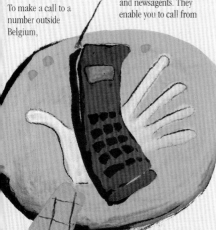

BUREAUX DE CHANGE

Banks in Brussels are open from 9am-4pm or 6pm Monday to Friday and some are also open on Saturdays from 9am–noon. The bureaux de change at the Gare du Midi (open every day 6.30am–10.30pm) and the Gare du Nord (open every day 7am-10pm) accept foreign currency, traveller's cheques and international credit cards (Visa, Eurocard and Mastercard) and charge a BF30 commission per transaction. Once in the city, try and change your money at a branch of the **GWK**, where you'll get a good rate (better than at a bank) and they don't charge commission. The branch at the Marché-aux-Herbes is open every day 9am-9.30pm. Watch out – the other bureaux de change around the Grand-Place charge a 10% commission per transaction and don't accept any cards. You can use your credit card in cash machines to withdraw money directly from your account. Although you have to pay commission

on the exchange, you'll get a good rate, similar to that of traveller's cheques. It's a good idea to take out a large sum each time, though, as commission is charged per transaction, and you should in any case make sure you have enough money before the weekend starts, as the machines often run out of money on Saturday. If you have an American Express card, you can cash a personal cheque at the branch at the Gare du Midi ☎ 556 3600, which is open every day from 6.30am–10pm.

TOURIST OFFICES

TIB (Brussels Tourist Information Office), Brussels Town Hall-Grand-Place-1000 ☎ 513 8940, ☎ 514 4538. Open every day 9am–6pm (Sunday 10am–2pm in winter), closed on Sundays in January and February and also on 1 January and 25 December.

Here you can get leaflets about cultural events in Brussels (the *BBB* weekly calendar), hotels and restaurants. The staff will

also book your hotel or tickets for you. The bookshop sells a very detailed guide to Brussels, including a map (BF80), a restaurant guide, suggested itineraries on different themes and a few interesting books on art and items of historical interest in Brussels.

OPT (Office for the Promotion of Tourism), 63, Rue du Marché-aux-Herbes-1000 ☎ 504 0390, ☎ 504 0270. Mon.–Fri. 9am-6pm (7pm Jul.–Aug.), Sat. 9am–1pm, 2–6pm (7pm Jul.–Aug.), Sun. 9am–1pm Nov.–Apr., 9am–1pm, 2–6pm Apr.–Oct. This office is more welcoming than the TIB and has a wide range of information on Brussels (city plan, metro map, general brochure, leaflets on museums and exhibitions and calendar of events) and Belgium as a whole. The staff are very friendly and will be only too plesed to answer your questions about which museums are open on Mondays or where to find a good vegetarian restaurant.

***Visit Brussels* Passport**
This card is valid for one year and can be bought at the TIB for BF300. It gives you a reduction on entrance charges at 18 museums, some exhibitions and other attractions. It also includes a day pass for public transport in Brussels and gives you a 60 % reduction on return tickets bought from the Belgian railway company. Ask for a *B-Excursion VB3* ticket at any station.

THEMED TOURS

For a special tour of Brussels, go to one of the organisations that run guided walks or bus tours, which generally last about 3 hours. Led by art historians, these are themed around Art Nouveau, Art Deco or the Industrial Heritage and will take you to places that are generally not open to the public, such as the Van Eetvelde hotel, the Horta house or the Art Deco swimming pool at the *Résidence Palace*. The Urban Transport museum runs a guided tour of the city on old-fashioned trams. It's a good idea to book in advance for all these tours.

L'Arau
☎ 219 3345
(Mon.–Fri. 9am–5pm).
Themed coach tours on Sat. and Sun.

Arcadia
☎ 534 3819
(Mon.–Fri. 9am–12.30pm, 2–6pm). Seven tours on foot or by coach on Sundays.

La Fonderie
☎ 410 9950
(Mon.–Fri. 9am–5pm).
From the Anderlecht abattoirs to maritime Brussels, these tours are by boat, coach or on foot on Sat. and Sun. from late May to October.

Le Bus Bavard
☎ 673 1835.
Every day at 10am from 15 Jun. to 15 Sep. A 3-hour walk round the city centre.

Provelo
☎ 502 7355.
Bicycle tours of 8–28 miles by day or night in and around Brussels, from Fri.–Sun. during Jun–Sep. and by arrangement the rest of the year.

Musée du Transport urbain (Urban Transport Museum), 364 b, Av. de Tervuren-1150
☎ 515 3107.
A 3-hour tour on a 1930s tram departs from the museum at 10am on Sundays and public holidays from May to September.

OPENING TIMES FOR MUSEUMS AND ATTRACTIONS

Most of the museums are open from 9 or 10am to 5 or 6pm. Museums are closed on Mondays. Remember that some museums close for lunch and that staff shortages may mean that others are open only in the afternoons or every other weekend. There are reductions for students, children aged 6-18 and senior citizens (over 60), so don't forget to pack your identity/proof of age cards before you leave.

USEFUL ADDRESSES

British Embassy
85, Rue d'Arlon 1040
☎ 287 6211

Police (emergency)
☎ 101

Central Police Station
30, Rue du Marché-au-Charbon
☎ 517 9611

Emergencies ☎ 100

Accidents ☎ 105

Duty doctor and chemist
☎ 479 1818

Emergency doctor
☎ 513 0202

Emergency dental service
☎ 426 1026

Breakdown service
☎ 070 344 777

Lost property
Zaventem airport
☎ 753 6820
Police ☎ 517 9695
Trains (Gare du Nord)
☎ 224 6112
Trams, buses, metro
☎ 515 2394

Îlot sacré

Guided by the crowds of tourists you'll have no trouble in finding the magnificent Grand-Place, a theatrical square filled with cafés. Once you've got over your wonder, try exploring the area's narrow streets, making sure you avoid hazards such as the restaurants in Rue des Bouchers and the

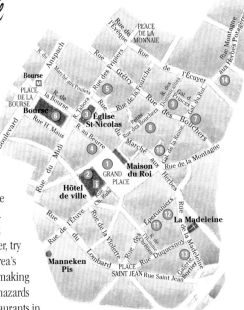

souvenir shops on the way to Mannekenpis. The upmarket shops, secondhand booksellers and friendly cafés where you can sample a glass of real gueuse beer are just around the corner, but don't go on a Sunday, because everything will be shut.

❶ Grand-Place

The inhabitants of Brussels have a taste for individualism and eclecticism, as shown by this magnificent group of corporation houses, rebuilt after the French bombardment of 1695. Flemish Italian-Spanish in style, the façades are crumbling under their

Baroque decorations and gilding. The 'richest theatre in the world' (according to French writer Jean Cocteau) is home to a bird market on

Sunday mornings and a magnificent revival of bygone splendours during the annual *Ommegang* festival, a re-enactment of the Joyous Entry of Emperor Charles V in 1549.

❷ Town Hall★★★
☎ 279 4365
Guided tours Tue. 10.45am and 2.30pm, Wed. 2.30pm and in summer Sun. 10.45am. Entry charge.

The only Gothic building on the square (the king's house opposite is a 19th-century pastiche), it was built in two stages, giving rise to a legend that the architect threw himself off the tower when he saw that the two wings were asymmetrical. St Michael, patron saint of the city, slays his dragon at the top of the carved stone steeple. Inside are some of the fine 17th- and 18th-century tapestries that made the reputation of the Brussels weavers.

❸ Church of St Nicolas★★

Along with the city hall this church, dedicated to the patron saint of merchants, with little houses clinging to its sides, is one of the few remnants of the Middle Ages. The butter market used to be held in front of it. The church is Gothic in style, with fine panelling and Louis XIV pews. Take a look at the *Virgin and Sleeping Child*, attributed to Rubens, on the left-hand pillar in front of the choir, and a cannonball buried in the stone, which is a remnant of the fighting in 1695.

❹ Dandoy Biscuit factory★★
31, Rue au Beurre
☎ 511 0326
Mon.-Sat. 8.30am-6.30pm, Sun. and holidays 10.30am-6.30pm.

A shop smelling wonderfully of cinnamon, almond and

butter. In this 17th-century house five generations of Dandoys have been making *speculoos, pains d'amandes, pain à la grecque* and marzipan cake flavoured with orange flower since 1829. Food lovers will be unable to resist, especially as the *speculoos* come in the shape of St Nicolas or a pot-bellied burgher.

❺ À la Bécasse★
11, Rue de Tabora
☎ 511 0006
Open every day 10-1am and 2am on Fri. and Sat.

If you fancy a glass of good *lambic* served with bread and cream cheese, hidden away at the end of this cul-de-sac you'll find this café, full of gleaming copper kegs. It's been here since 1877 and is one of the last establishments that still sells draught *lambic* and *kriek*. Two varieties of *lambic, doux* (sweet) or *blanc* (white), are served in stoneware jugs and it's renowned for being a potent brew!

❻ The Bourse★

Built by Léon Suys (1873) on the site of the Des Récollets convent, this is one of the key buildings in the Anspach city

plan. Its façade looks like a Roman temple weighed down with Baroque decorations, reflecting the wealth of a young and rapidly growing nation. The sculptors whose work decorates the building include the young Rodin, who is supposed to have contributed to the allegorical groups of *Asia* and *Africa*.

❼ Galeries Royales Saint-Hubert★★★

Since it opened in 1847 the city's most elegant passage has been a meeting-place for Brussels' high society. Housed

between the pilasters under its vast glass roof are huge apartments, concert halls, luxury shops, antique shops and the only two restaurants worthy of the name in this district, the *Ogenblik* and the *Taverne du Passage*.

❽ Théâtre de Toone★★
6, Impasse Schuddeveld-Rue des Bouchers
☎ **513 5486**
Performances at 8.30pm Tue. to Sat.

For an unusual experience how about *Le Cid*, *Othello* or *The Three Musketeers* performed in the Brussels' dialect by puppets? These shows have been running for 170 years. Like Woltje, MC Toone VII, alias José Géal, has all the characteristic arrogance and rebellious spirit of the true *Brusseleir*. The show continues in the café next door.

❾ Tropismes★★
11, Gal. des Princes
☎ **512 8852**
Sun. and Mon. 1.30-6.30pm, Tue.-Thu. 10am-6.30pm, Fri. 10am-8pm, Sat. 10.30am-6.30pm.

A 19th-century cabaret venue, all gold, stucco, columns and mirrors is now home to one of the city's largest bookshops, specialising in literature and the social sciences. Literary gatherings are held here, maintaining Brussels' traditional role as an intellectual centre, which it acquired when French writers Victor Hugo and Charles Baudelaire were in exile here.

❿ Manufacture Belge de Dentelles★
6-8, Gal. de la Reine, Galerie Royale Saint-Hubert
☎ **511 4477**
Mon.-Sat. 9am-6pm, Sun. 10am-4pm (closed Sun. in Nov. and Feb.).

If you like lace make sure you step inside this venerable shop which has been supplying Brussels' high society with wedding veils and christening gowns since 1810. Here, depending on how much you want to pay, you can buy lace that's either entirely hand-made, or hand-stitched on a machine-produced template. It's also worth asking to see the pieces in their special collection.

⓫ Plaizier★★
50, Rue des Éperonniers
☎ **513 4730**
Tue.-Sat. 11am-1pm, 3-6pm.

Here you can treat yourself to a fascinating series of 1930s views of Brussels in the rain, a *hecho en Mexico* diary, a miniature reproduction of Hoffmann's *Sitzmachine*, a dictionary of pictogrammes for serious travellers, or even that great book by Dr Alan Francis *Sex after 50*!

⓬ La Courte Échelle★
12, Rue des Éperonniers
☎ **512 4759**
11am-1.30pm and 2-6pm, closed Wed. and Sun.

This is a paradise for Lilliputians. There are houses just their size and everything that goes inside, from furniture to food and the china to eat it from. Items include crystal chandeliers, oriental carpets, toys, a goldfish bowl; in other words the whole world in miniature, which will fascinate young and old alike. There's absolutely everything you could ever imagine, including corsets for the little ladies.

⓭ Galerie Bortier★★
Tue.-Sat. 10am-6.30pm.

At the Rue de la Madeleine end, this narrow covered passage has a façade in the Flemish Baroque style and is decorated inside with cast-iron ornaments. This is a world of muffled quiet, where serious collectors of old books and engravings mingle with ordinary browsers looking for a secondhand book.

⓮ À la Mort Subite★
7, Rue Montagne-aux-Herbes-Potagères
☎ 513 1318
Open every day
10.30-1am.

This long café, with its walls stained by generations of smokers is a Brussels institution, where you can sample a generous gueuse beer known as *Mort Subite* or 'Sudden Death'. If you're a beer connoisseur, why not order a *Faro*, a one-year-old *lambic* sweetened with candy sugar and caramel.

PAIN À LA GRECQUE, A BRUSSELS SPECIALITY

'Greek-style bread' is a strange name for a biscuit that has been made in Brussels since the 16th century! In fact the recipe didn't come from the Greeks but from the monks of the Fossé aux Loups monastery and originally consisted of a long loaf which was covered in sugar on feast days. The name *Bruut van de grecht* must have been too hard to pronounce for the French soldiers who occupied the city in the 17th century. They called it *pain à la grecque*, but the recipe has stayed the same.

Saint-Géry
birthplace of the city

I t was here that *'Bruocsella'* ('the house in the marsh') was founded in 979, when Charles of France built a *castrum* with an oratory dedicated to St Géry on a small island covered in wild irises, nestling in a meander of the Senne. This district suffered badly from the greed of property developers around the 1970s, but is now gradually being revived thanks to the dynamism of its inhabitants, who have turned it into the trendiest place in central Brussels. Along with the gay clubs you'll find shops selling avant-garde fashions by Belgian designers and restaurants and cafés with wild and wacky interiors.

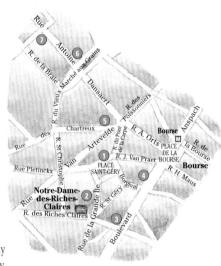

❶ Place Saint-Géry★★

The hour of revenge has come for St Géry. Although his church, now buried under the great hall of the meat market (1881), will never see the light of day again, the square dedicated to him is once more a popular and thriving area. On the brightly coloured façades of the old buildings you can read the story of a district whose heart beats strongly, mostly at night.

❷ Notre-Dame-des-Riches-Claires★

A fine example of the architecture of the Flemish Renaissance (1665), the church of the St Clare nuns with its huge hemispherical dome has strange gables with decorative scrolls over the ends of the transept and choir. During restoration works after the fire of 1989, remains were uncovered dating back to the Roman period.

❸ Man to Man★
9, Rue des Riches-Claires
☎ **514 0296**
Tue.-Sat. 10am-6.30pm.

Ladies, don't bother stepping into this hairdresser's if you

want a perm. Apart from the whips and nipple clamps, all the S&M accessories on display in the window are for men only, unless you go in for latex G-strings and leather chaps. As for the boys, we'd better warn you that crew cuts are the house speciality.

❹ Kladaradatsch ! Palace★★★
85, Bd Anspach
☎ **501 6776**
Open every day noon-midnight.

The old Pathé Palace cinema, built in 1913, has had its gilding and its original purpose of showing films restored. As well as being a 'miniplex' for avant-garde cinema, this magnificent building, a stunning mix of Art Deco and neo-Classical styles, is the perfect place to meet a friend for a drink or something to eat. All in all, it's the new place to be seen in central Brussels.

❺ Le Greenwich★★
7, Rue des Chartreux
☎ **511 4167**
Open every day 11am-2pm.

This café has hardly changed at all since it opened at the end of the 19th century with its dark panelling, marble tables, glass roof and an old National cash register. The interior has inspired many film-makers, including Delvaux, and regulars once included the painter Magritte, who was a fanatical chess-player. Although it's lively in the evenings, the hushed atmosphere in the afternoons is the perfect aid to

concentration and the players are mostly on sparkling water. But there's nothing to stop you ordering a glass of Trappiste.

❻ RUE ANTOINE-DANSAERT: DOWNTOWN BRUSSELS

RUE ANTOINE DANSAERT STRAAT → 104

It's in this street, where 18th-century working people's houses are mixed in with massive 19th-century apartment blocks built for the bourgeoisie, that the avant-garde of Belgian fashion has chosen to locate their shops. You'll find their minimalist interiors alongside Baroque restaurants whose trendy customers don't necessarily have good food at the top of their list of priorities.

❼ Stijl★★★
74, Rue A.-Dansaert
☎ **512 0313**
Mon.-Sat. 10.30am-6.30pm.

This great shop, the showcase for the Antwerp designers (Ann Demeulemeester, Dries Van Noten, Dirk Bikkembergs and Raf Simons), has livened up the district all by itself. Very trendy clothing for men and women, exclusive, expensive, but very good quality. There's also a collection by David Fielden for brides who want an original wedding dress.

Sainte-Catherine
the old dock district

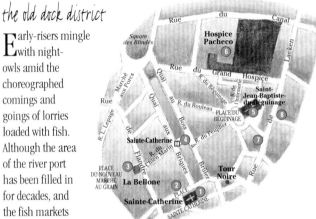

Early-risers mingle with night-owls amid the choreographed comings and goings of lorries loaded with fish. Although the area of the river port has been filled in for decades, and the fish markets have all been bulldozed, most of the locals are still engaged in the seafood trade. This area is particularly pleasant on fine days, when the pavements are covered in tables and chairs and musicians give impromptu concerts.

❶ Place Sainte-Catherine★
The lovely gabled façades and trees shading the square

almost make you forget the heavy forms of its 'neo-Gothic-Renaissance' church. Stop off at Martine's to taste the *caricoles* (whelks) or sample the wares of the mussel-sellers (from mid-July to mid-April), which the locals eat with bread and butter.

❷ La Belle Maraîchère★★
11A, Pl. Sainte-Catherine
☎ 512 9759
Fri.-Tue. noon-2.30pm and 6-10pm.

Easily the best value for money in the area. For 40 years Freddy Devreker has been delighting his customers' tastebuds with dishes that skilfully combine fish and shellfish. Terrine of ray and crab, scallops with *Noilly Prat*, superb fish soup and grilled turbot with hop shoots when they're in season. The desserts are just as delicious and you'll be given a very warm welcome.

❸ La Bellone★★★
46, Rue de Flandre
☎ 513 3333
Tue.-Fri. 10am-7pm, closed in July
Free entry.

Step through the porch and you'll discover a little gem in the Baroque style. This splendid patrician house dates from 1697 and is dedicated to Bellona, the Roman goddess of war. In 1980 the building became a venue for performances and is also a place for meetings and discussions. It has a reference library, and sometimes performances are staged in the courtyard.

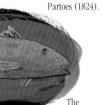

which dates from 1676, is a gem of Flemish Baroque and the narrow streets laid out in a star shape around it offer a haven of peace. Inside the church you'll find paintings in the style of Caravaggio by Van Loon, confession boxes guarded by angels and a stunning 18th-century pulpit dedicated to St Dominic.

8 DROGUERIE LE LION★★

55, Rue de Laeken
☎ **217 4202**
Mon.-Fri. 8.30am-5.30pm, Sat. 9am-noon.

Pure poetry – a wonderful combination of sights and fragrances. The great glass jars contain pigments of every colour, from burnt umber to scarlet, while the treasures hidden away in the wooden drawers include centaury flowers, artemisia and oregano. Mme Billet is always at the counter ready to give you her help and advice.

4 The old fish market★

Also known as *Vismet*, this group of pools is all that remains of the river port, which was abandoned in the 19th century. The fish market hall

(1883), a magnificent construction of cast iron and glass, was demolished in 1955 as the result of an absurd decision on the part of the authorities. The fish market is now held (4am-1pm) in the wholesalers' warehouses that line the old quays. Take a look at the lovely gabled houses, particularly *Le Cheval Marin*.

5 Saint-Jean-Baptiste-du-Béguinage★★★

This is one of those magical places where time seems to have stood still. The church,

6 Hospice Pacheco★★

The gardens of the Béguinage behind the church have given way to a fine group of neo-Classical buildings by Henri Partoes (1824).

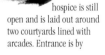

The hospice is still open and is laid out around two courtyards lined with arcades. Entrance is by

request and you can visit the first courtyard and the circular chapel with its coffered dome.

7 La Tentation★★
28 Rue de Laeken
☎ **223 2275**
Tue.-Sun. 11am-midnight, closed Sun. evening, Membership (FB200) gives admission to all concerts.

It was the Spanish Celts who organised the superb restoration of this former fabric shop, famous in our grandmothers' time. A magnificent Art Nouveau wrought-iron staircase, cast-iron pillars, *azulejo* tiles and a polished wood floor provide the setting for a café-restaurant serving *tapas* and Galician specialities. On Friday evenings you can hear a concert of world music and maybe also sample *Queimada*, a magic potion concocted by a real druid.

Place de Brouckère
the Brussels of the Belle Epoque

It was Bourgmestre Anspach's 19th-century dream of bringing magnificence to Brussels that led to the burial of the Senne river and the transformation of a working-class neighbourhood into a Parisian-style boulevard, lined with magnificent private residences. In those days Place de Brouckère was frequented by the new bourgeoisie, who dined at the *Métropole* after the theatre. Today it's caught between two opposing forces; the sex and fast-food industries are invading from the north, while to the south the luxury shops are slowly returning, trying to restore some of the area's former glory. If you raise your eyes above the neon signs you'll certainly see some stunning façades.

❶ Place de Brouckère★

In the days when it boasted expensive cafés, brasseries, grand hotels, theatres and the first cinema, this was one of the city's most fashionable areas. The construction of two 'American-style' towers in 1967 destroyed the harmony of the square, leaving the way open to an anarchic invasion of downmarket shops. The recent renovation of the Art Deco theatre of the Eldorado cinema and the refacing of some fine façades may mean the long-awaited revival is under way.

❷ Hôtel Métropole★★★
31, Pl. de Brouckère
☎ 217 2300.

Nothing changes this grand hotel. The passing of the years and crowned heads haven't left a mark on it. The café terrace is always full, summer and winter, while a nostalgic feel to the Belle Époque lounges is reminiscent of the Orient Express.

❸ Passage du Nord★
1, Bd A.-Max.

At the beginning of the old Boulevard du Nord is a passage (1881) decorated with caryatids – columns in the shape of female figures. The architect was inspired by the lovely building next door called 'Hier ist den kater en de kat', which won first prize for architecture in 1872. The exclusive shops have all moved out but oyster connoisseurs still visit the *Oyster bar* (Mon.-Sat. 11am-7pm) to enjoy Zélande oysters at the counter, washed down with a glass of white wine.

❹ 100 % Design★★
30, Bd Anspach
☎ 219 6198
Tue.-Sat. 10am-6.30pm and Mon. noon-6.30pm.

This is the place to buy inflatable furniture and decorative items for your home – if you've got the puff! Besides the classic chairs and stools you'll find wastepaper baskets, photo frames, clocks and even tulips full of air. There are floating fish to keep

your water-bound ones company and plastic Ron Arad shelving you can arrange any way you like, all at good prices.

❺ Théâtre de la Monnaie★★
☎ 229 1372

Guided tours Sat. at noon from late Aug. to late June.

Founded in 1700 this is Belgium's finest venue, hosting performances of work by Béjart and his 20th-century ballet from 1960 to 1989. Architecturally it's a mixture of styles: the façade dates from the

Napoleonic era, the 'neo-Baroque' hall and royal box were designed by Pœlaert, while the foyer was decorated by two American conceptual artists, Sol LeWitt and Sam Francis.

❻ Rue Neuve★
A few mime artists perform to the crowds of stylish young people who rush from shop to shop and the heady smell of hot waffles is irresistible. This is the busiest pedestrian street in Brussels, particularly on a Saturday. Here you can dress yourself cheaply from head to toe as long as you like T-shirts, bright colours and platform shoes.

❼ Place des Martyrs★★

This square of bourgeois residences built in the late 18th century in the purest neo-Classical style was one of the city's finest squares before becoming the sad symbol of linguistic quarrelling. In the 1960s it was left to go to rack and ruin, before finally being renovated in the 'façadism' manner. On one side are the offices of the Flemish presidency, on the other the theatre of the French-speaking community.

Coudenberg, the royal mountain

Coudenberg, located halfway between the upper and lower cities, has been a residence of princes since the 11th century. You may not be able to shop here, but you can fill up on culture in one of its four museums, catch a

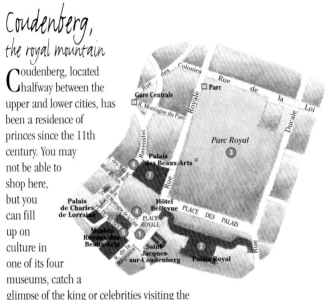

glimpse of the king or celebrities visiting the palace, go for a jog round the park or listen to a concert at the Palais des Beaux-Arts. Best of all you'll get a superb view over Grand-Place from the top of the Mont des Arts.

❶ Place Royale★★★

This elegant neo-Classical square, with its statue of Godefroy de Bouillon, is the work of Charles de Lorraine. Enter the arcade to the left of the Museum of Modern Art to explore the fine Louis XVI style palace, whose wings close off the view of the museum square.

❷ Palais Royal★★

The Louis XVI façade, modified under Leopold II, hides two bourgeois residences built in the 18th century. The building is very grand, but the king only comes here for official occasions. At the end of the gallery on the right is the Hôtel Bellevue, former home to upper-class residents, whose period salons now host exhibitions of furniture and valuable objects (museum open Tue.-Sun. 10am-4pm).

❸ Parc Royal★

These lovely grounds, laid out in the French style over 13 ha/32 acres, were designed by B. Guimard in 1775. As you walk along the tree-lined avenues you'll come upon a great many sculptures with mythological subjects, artificial lakes and delightful pavilions where concerts are staged in summer.

4 Magasins Old England★
3, Rue Montagne-de-la-Cour.

With its metal scrolls overhanging the street, the frivolity of this superb Art Nouveau building designed by Saintenoy in 1899 contrasts with its sober neighbours. It's recently become home to the Instrument Museum, which has one of the world's richest collections, including the instruments invented by Adolphe Sax.

5 Musées Royaux des Beaux-Arts★★★
3, Rue de la Régence
☎ 508 3211
**Tue.-Sun. 10am-5pm;
Period Art closed noon-1pm
and Modern Art closed
1-2pm. Entry charge.**

These museums offer a vast panorama of painting and sculpture in Belgium from the Middle Ages to recent times. Make sure you see the Flemish primitives, Brueghels and Rubens, in the period section. The underground

gallery in the Modern Art section (opened in 1984) is an architectural feat created by Bastin. Make sure you don't miss Spilliaert's sea paintings, the Flemish expressionists and the Surrealist works by Delvaux and Magritte.

6 La Boîte à Musique★★
17, Rue Ravenstein
☎ 513 0965
Mon.-Sat. 9.30am-6.30pm.

This is the only shop in the city specialising in recordings of classical music, with an impressive 20,000 titles to choose from. It's also the home of an independent producer, *Pavane Records*. It's an ideal place for music lovers, who can buy either directly, by mail order or on the internet.

PALACE OF THE DUKES OF BURGUNDY

For once the large hole in the Place Royale isn't one of Brussels' long-term building sites; it's an archeological dig started in 1995. The remains being excavated are those of the Aula Magna, part of the palace built by Philip the Good, Duke of Burgundy. The palace was destroyed on the night of 3 February 1731 in a terrible fire started by the cooks, who were too busy making jam to notice!

7 Palais des Beaux-Arts★★
23, Rue Ravenstein
☎ 507 8200
Box office Mon.-Sat. 11am-6pm.

This centre of cultural life houses a vast concert hall with amazing acoustics, a theatre and exhibition spaces. It was also one of Horta's last designs. He was still setting the trend in 1922 with his pure lines heralding Art Deco and his extensive use of concrete. Each year the prestigious Queen Elisabeth competition is held here.

Sablon
a trip round the antique shops

Sablon's streets are lined with the city's best antique shops, its flea market is the busiest in Brussels and the terraces of its smart cafés are always crowded. An absolute must for your weekend, it's the place to catch the latest hits, get the name of the most fashionable clubs or taste some of Wittamer's incomparable cakes. And if it's antiques you're after, you'll find some fine things at quite reasonable prices.

❶ Place du Grand-Sablon★★

The magnificent 17th- and 18th-century façades set the scene for the antiques market which is held here every weekend (Sat. 9am-6pm and Sun. 9am-2pm). Since the wealthy Eurocrats arrived it's been hard to unearth a bargain here, but it's still a great place to wander around.

❷ Notre-Dame-du-Sablon★★★

A small boat depicted above the south door is a reminder that in 1348 this was the

mode of transport used to bring the miraculous statue of the Virgin Mary to the church of the crossbowmen's guild. Unusually this jewel of the Brabant flamboyant Gothic style has internal flying buttresses. On 3 November a hunting horn calls the faithful to a special mass celebrating the feast-day of St Hubert.

❸ Square du Petit-Sablon★

This is a delightful little park, is full of flowers and lovely to walk in. In the centre is a group sculpture showing Count d'Egmont and Count de Hornes, heroes of the resistance to the Spanish occupiers, with ten 16th-century humanists standing around them in a semi-circle. The attributes of 48 corporate bodies are represented on the iron railings round the park. See if you can identify them!

4 Palais d'Egmont★★
Garden only open to the public (entrance on Rue du Grand-Cerf).

This magnificent 18th-century aristocratic residence, which closes off the view of Sablons, was home to the d'Egmont and d'Arenberg families before being turned over to the Ministry of Foreign Affairs. The garden contains two *Ginkgo biloba* trees and a tulip tree.

5 Postal Service Museum★★
**40, Pl. du Grand-Sablon
☎ 511 7740
Tue.-Sat. 10am-4.30pm.**

Besides a complete collection of Belgian postage stamps from 1849 to the present day, this neo-Classical former residence of the de Masmine princes houses machines, models, costumes and other objects relating to the history of the postal service in Belgium and the Congo. Portraits of the Tassis, inventors of the postal service in 1501, amazing postilions'

boots weighing over 8 kg/17 lbs, a post horn and a 1900 office are just a few of the items in this fascinating museum.

6 Écailler du Palais Royal★
**18, Rue Bodenbroek
☎ 512 8751
Lunch and evenings., closed Sun., hols. and Aug.**

A cosy interior with blue mosaics, where you will be served succulent dishes based on fish and shellfish, given two stars in the *Michelin Guide*. Besides dishes such as curried lobster ravioli and John Dory *au beurre blanc*, the *plat du jour* is always worth trying. Be prepared for a fairly large bill.

7 Impasse Saint-Jacques★
**Dartevelle, nos 8-9,
☎ 513 0175
Mon.-Sat. 10am-6pm.
Tribal Arms, no. 15,
☎ 511 4767, Sat. 10am-7pm and Sun. 10am-4pm.
Ambre Congo, no. 17, ☎ 511 1662, Tue.-Fri. 10am-12.30pm and 2.30pm-6pm, Sat. 11am-1pm and 3-6.30pm**

Although it has lost some charm since the Hôtel Jolly was built, this is still a haunt for dealers in ethnic objects. Africa is the main source of the items in the shop owned by Unesco expert Dartevelle, while the little shop at the end of the cul-de-sac specialises in tribal weapons.

8 Wittamer★★
12-13, Pl. du Grand-Sablon
☎ 512 3742
Mon. 10am-6pm, Tue.-Sat.
7am-7pm, Sun. 7am-6.30pm.

The home of delicious cakes, good bread and Viennese pastries since 1910, this shop is so successful that Henri Wittamer (the third) has also opened a cake shop at no. 6. You can either eat your *samba* chocolate cake, meringue soufflé with fresh fruit or *couques aux raisins* in the shop or take away.

9 Rosalie Pompon★
65, Rue Lebeau
☎ 512 3593
Tue.-Sat. 10.30am-6pm
and Sun. 11am-5pm.

If you're really short of gift ideas, you won't leave this shop empty-handed. From waterlily-leaf umbrellas with dangling frogs to Wallace and Gromit radios, hairslides covered in fake Smarties to CD racks shaped like birdcages. Things to suit every purse, from BF250.

10 Vienna★★★
14, Rue Watteeu
☎ 503 1520
Tue.-Fri. 2-6pm, Sat.
11am-6pm.

If you love exclusive objects and furniture with pure lines, make sure you visit this shop. All the great names of the Viennese Secession (Hoffmann, Moser, Wagner), Belgian

Art Nouveau (Horta, Van de Velde, Hankar, Serrurier-Bovy) and modernist Art Deco are represented here in this beautiful setting. All the pieces on sale here are of exceptional quality and there's something to suit every pocket, from an Art Deco alarm clock to the *Siztmachine*.

11 Marie Storms★★
13, Rue de Rollebeek
☎ 511 7314
Tue.-Thu. and Sat. 11am-6pm and Fri. by appt.

If you've always dreamed of wearing the jewellery of Battista Sforza or Isabelle d'Este, step inside Marie Storms' superb shop. Her inspiration comes from the Italian renaissance and her glass beads from Murano.

Powdered gold blown onto lapis lazuli, baroque strings of pearls, byzantine necklaces, antique cameos, in other words jewels fit for a queen, at very reasonable prices. A favourite shop of the Belgian upper classes, including Queen Paola.

12 Galerie Yannick David★★★
27, Rue Watteeu
☎ 513 3748
Tue.-Sat. 11am-1pm
and 2-6pm.

A shop for lovers of unusual or bizarre objects, for curious browsers, keen collectors or indeed anyone who might be looking for a tiny 17th-century inlaid commode that won't take up too much space in a studio apartment! Alongside a walnut model of a church tower made by two skilled craftsmen, you might find a miniature carpenter's bench or stunning pieces of furniture made with Lilliputians in mind.

CELEBRATIONS IN SABLON

In April the baroque music festival infiltrates the churches and antique shops; in June the galleries of primitive and ethnic art open their doors to foreign exhibitors; in July the Ommegang procession sets off from the church of Notre-Dame; while in December the giant Christmas market lights up the entire square.

⑬ Cento Anni★★
31, Pl. du Grand-Sablon
☎ 514 5633, 075 300 200
Tue.-Sat. 11am-1pm and 2.30-6pm, Sun. 11am-2pm.

Rodrigo Diaz specialises in European

Art Deco and Art Nouveau objects and small pieces of furniture. It's here that you'll find sublime *pâte de verre,* a Secession pedestal table, a silver tea service or very rare pieces of signed or marked jewellery from around 1900.

⑭ Church of Sts-Jean-et-Étienne-aux-Minimes★★
Concerts at 10.30am; services at 11.30am on Sun.

The Italian-style façade with its pilasters (1715) hints at the beautiful order and light of the classical interior. Besides the Gregorian chants sung during Sunday mass, the church regularly hosts concerts of music by Bach and Handel.

⑮ Le Perroquet★
31, Rue Watteeu
☎ 512 9922
Open every day 10.30am-1.30pm.

Inside you'll find chequered floor tiles, stained glass, gently filtered light and a carved wooden counter. Outside, the pavement tables are seized as soon as the first ray of sunlight appears. At any time you'll find an enormous choice of *pitas* and a few healthy salads. You can also enjoy a glass of wine in this lovely Art Nouveau bistrot.

Marolles
a working-class area

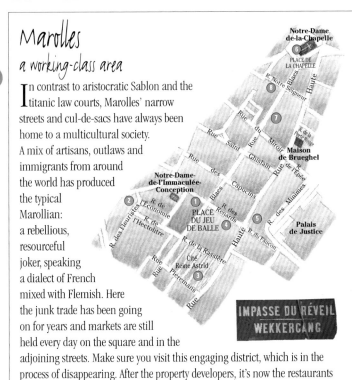

In contrast to aristocratic Sablon and the titanic law courts, Marolles' narrow streets and cul-de-sacs have always been home to a multicultural society. A mix of artisans, outlaws and immigrants from around the world has produced the typical Marollian: a rebellious, resourceful joker, speaking a dialect of French mixed with Flemish. Here the junk trade has been going on for years and markets are still held every day on the square and in the adjoining streets. Make sure you visit this engaging district, which is in the process of disappearing. After the property developers, it's now the restaurants and fashionable clubs that are threatening its existence.

❶ Place du Jeu-de-Balle ★★★
Bric-a-brac every day, 7am-2pm.

At 5am an enormous pile of disparate objects is unpacked and the collectors swoop. Amongst all the rubbish you can sometimes unearth a real bargain. On Sundays they take more care over the presentation, and the prices too. The best time for bargain hunters is on Tuesdays or first thing on a Friday morning, but it's entertaining at any time to catch the Brussels' *zwanze* and watch deals being struck in Arabic.

❷ Modes ★★
3, Rue des Fleuristes
☎ **512 4907**
Wed.-Sun. 10am-2pm, Tue. 10am-1pm.

In this shop you'll meet film wardrobe mistresses and designers in search of inspiration. All the clothes and accessories here date from before 1950 and are in very good condition. It's just the place to find a complete old-fashioned trousseau, a felt purse, a ball gown from the 1930s or lovely pieces of costume jewellery.

❸ Cité Reine-Astrid ★
When they were built in 1914 these blocks of flats, arranged in six parallel rows, were at the cutting edge of avant-garde social housing. Hygiene,

light and functionality were the watchwords of the builders of these coloured brick constructions, now mainly inhabited by people of North African origin, who have brought their own unique style to the buildings.

❹ Antoni Jassogne★★
21, Rue des Renards
☎ 511 8514
Mon.-Sat. 10.30am-7pm.

Pause for an moment to admire the precise workmanship of these stringed instruments. Take in the subtle aroma of maple and spruce, the tools with polished handles on the bench and the violins waiting to be played. A violin made here costs around BF300,000.

❺ Café Alex★
224, Rue Haute
☎ 514 2288
9.30-2.30am, closed Wed.

This is the *stamcafé* frequented by the old men of

the area, one of the last they still feel at home in. Jokes in *Brusseleir* between sips of *Maes*, slices of life revealed in a nickname, and an owner with a big moustache who'll tell you the secrets of *blœmpanch*. It's best to go in the morning and don't forget to admire the Art Deco furniture and stained glass, here since the café opened in 1926.

❻ Notre-Dame-de-la-Chapelle★★

A strange Baroque tower rises above the old parish of the painter Brueghel the Elder, who's buried here. The 13th-century Romano-Gothic core has been extended over the years, but this in no way mars one of the city's most beautiful churches.

❼ Apostrophe ★★★

50, Rue Blaes
☎ 502 6738
Mon.-Sat. 10am-6pm, Sun. 10am-3.30pm.

This is the meeting place of curious travellers and

collectors of bizarre objects. The shop specialises in old trade furniture (from 1880 to 1930) and unusual objects, from a grocer's shop counter to rows of office drawers and chemist's cupboards. The prices are as welcoming as the reception.

❽ La Grande Porte★
9, Rue Notre-Seigneur
☎ 512 8998
Mon.-Sat. noon-3pm, 6pm-2am. Closed Sat. lunchtimes.

Here you sit at a bare table to eat your nourishing *stœmp*, stew with beer or chicken with *Kriek*. The worn floor tiles, paper lanterns and pianola have been here for ages, as have the regulars. There is a warm, friendly atmosphere and food is served until 2am.

Saint-Gilles
the Art Nouveau manifesto

This is an elegant business district, with a great number of Art Nouveau houses. This anti-rational, exuberant style, thought shocking when the houses were built, was adopted by the new bourgeois industrialists, who commissioned the best architects to build their private residences. Today their sensual façades conceal offices and a few good restaurants; but if you really want to plunge into the world of the visionary Art Nouveau architect Horta, make sure you go on a tour of his private house. The area is at its liveliest on Wednesday afternoons, due to the market held on Place du Châtelain.

❶ Musée Horta★★★
25, Rue Américaine
☎ 537 1692
Tue.-Sun. 2-5.30pm
Entry charge.

Victor Horta's private house and the studio next door are a catalogue of the skills of a man for whom simply being a brilliant architect wasn't enough. In addition to the spectacular staircase, lit by a golden-brown skylight, this is the only house to have retained its original interior decor and furniture.

❷ La Quincaillerie★★★
45, Rue du Page
☎ 538 2553

Open every day except Sat. and Sun. lunchtimes.

Wooden drawers from floor to ceiling, a *Temps Modernes* clock and wrought iron characterise this former Art Nouveau hardware store, now a brasserie. All the food is made with fresh ingredients, style and skill. Choose from fresh oysters or special dishes, divine home-made desserts and a good wine list. All the staff are women, and the diners tend to be lawyers and people in fashion or advertising.

❸ À la Page★★

72, Rue du Page
☎ 538 3396
Mon.-Sat. 11am-6.30pm.

Everything is deliciously retro in this little shop with its old-fashioned charm, iron stove and embroidered linen overflowing out of old chests. Clothes from our mothers' and grandmothers' day on the rails, some used, some not, for both sexes as well as for children. Have a look in the shop next door (*Côte à Côte*) specialising in 1900-1950s bric-a-brac.

❹ Thiérry Boutemy★★★

81, Rue du Magistrat
☎ 649 3949
Tue.-Sat. 11am-7pm.

Once inside you're instantly plunged into a world of delicately scented wood, with polished furniture, crystal chandeliers, Baroque mouldings, polished pebbles and armfuls of fresh cut flowers. This is the lair of a talented florist who knows all the secrets of flowers.

❺ Santosh★

47, Pl. du Châtelain
☎ 647 2227
Mon.-Sat. 10am-6pm.

Here you'll find lovely objects too big to bring back in your luggage from a trip to India: statues of Hindu gods, carved screens, painted cupboards and coloured candlesticks, all superbly presented. There are also some very beautiful clothes made of silk or cotton, original designs which go very well with Indian jewellery.

❻ La Septième Tasse★

37, Rue du Bailli
☎ 647 1971
Thu.-Mon. 11am-7.30pm.

Sixty varieties of tea and as many different teapots, all unearthed in bric-a-brac stalls, serve up a perfumed brew that will transport you to a Chinese paradise. From the pretty garden to the tearoom lined in pale wood, this is the perfect place to sooth your aching feet and any pangs of thirst and hunger. Connoisseurs can enjoy such delights as *maté* (Paraguay tea).

❼ Peinture Fraîche★★

10, Rue du Tabellion
☎ 537 1105
Tue.-Sat. 11am-7pm.

Settled in the square in front of the Trinité church for over 10 years, this friendly little bookshop specialises in 20th-century architecture, photography, graphic design and fine art. The shelves are full of enticing books and you'll always get a warm welcome.

8 Le Framboisier Doré★★
35, Rue du Bailli
☎ 647 5144
Tue.-Fri. 11.30am-11pm (8pm in winter), Sat.-Sun. 12.30-11pm (8pm in winter).

Fresh milk, eggs, vanilla pods and fruit are combined to make wonderful old-fashioned ice-cream. The ice-cream-maker's creative imagination will take you down uncharted paths. From flowers to Sauternes and gueuze, there are 200 flavours to try in this pretty café which also serves waffles, cakes and hot chocolate.

9 Hôtel Tassel★★★
6, Rue Paul-Émile Janson.

A glass bow window set in yellow and blue stone, continuous, flowing lines, small columns bursting out of the stone and a curving balustrade. All the themes of Horta's architectural language can be seen here, in his second design for a private residence (1893), created for his friend Professor Tassel.

10 T'Aka Gallery★
84, Rue de Livourne
☎ 538 2538
Tue.-Sat. 12-6.30pm.

The pieces of jewellery, leather goods, ceramics and clothes on display in this shop all have one thing in common – they were designed by artists not only from Brussels, but from all over the world. From the Baroque jewellery by Stefano Poletti, a designer for Christian Lacroix, to the betel-leaf boxes from Timor, the choice is as wide as the price range.

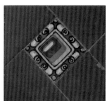

11 Centre Culturel Art Média★★★
14, Rue Defacqz
☎ 544 0833
Open every day 10am-6pm, weekends by appointment.

The slightly Moorish façade hides a stunning exercise in Andalusian style. It's the work of Adrien Blomme, commissioned in 1925 by the brewer Wielemans to re-create a Granada *casa*. The rooms, laid out around a patio tiled entirely in *guardillas* and other *azulejos*, host prestigious exhibitions, a library and document centre, a bookshop and a children's workshop. Outside there's a fairy-tale garden.

12 Ciamberlani and Janssens houses★★
48-50, Rue Defacqz.

These two very different buildings (1897-98) designed by Paul Hankar have an impressive sobriety unusual in Art Nouveau design. Hankar exploited the ornamental possibilities of combining brick, stone and multi-coloured sgraffiti (*see right*). Note the horseshoe openings, which are his trademark.

⓭ Hôtel Otlet★
48, Rue de Livourne.

The abandonment of symmetry in favour of a clever interplay of lines moving inwards and outwards reflects Octave Van Rysselberghe's desire to fit into the Art Nouveau movement. Comparing this building with the Hôtel Tassel, built at the same time, you sense a certain timidity on the architect's part, though his building is still elegant.

⓮ The Amadeus Restaurant and Wine Bar★★
13, Rue Veydt
☎ 538 3427
Restaurant open every day except Sat. lunchtime; bar Tue.-Sat. 6.30pm-1.30am.

This restaurant with its separate wine bar has a film-set interior, with its chandeliers, candles, high-ceilinged

rooms, mirrors and courtyard. Relax and enjoy the classical music in the background as you sample the wine list. A perfect setting for a romantic meal, this used to be Rodin's studio. The menu comprises modern and typical Belgian cuisine, such as *waterzooi* and there are a couple of vegetarian dishes on offer too. It can be a little pricey, but the setting more than makes up for it. They do a popular brunch on Sundays from 10am-12pm.

SGRAFFITI

Sgraffiti, which were very fashionable in the late 19th century to decorate Art Nouveau façades, are wall decorations taken from the Italian Renaissance. A pale-coloured wash is applied over a mix of mortar and ash, and then carved with ornamental designs and figures. Artists often drew the designs onto paper first, then transferred them to the façade by means of a toothed tracing wheel. Unlike frescos, the colours of sgraffiti are applied in several layers.

Around Place Brugmann
a relaxing place to shop

Take the number 60 bus and explore the beautiful avenues lined with trees and smart houses in the Parisian and Art Nouveau styles. This is village Brussels, where everyone knows everyone else and all are keen to achieve the good life. You'd have to be crazy to go shopping elsewhere when all the best stores for the home, clothes, flowers and antiques are here. Stop off for refreshment at a little restaurant or milk bar and, with most shops open on Sunday, what more could you ask for?

❶ Scènes de Ménage★★★
4, Pl. Brugmann
☎ 344 3295
Tue.-Sat. 10.30am-6.30pm and Mon. 2-6.30pm.

It's a real feat in this cramped space to create so many different ambiances to display objects for the table and bathroom. Antique and modern are combined with impeccable taste. The place to find a horn caviar spoon, toothpicks with a shell decoration or Victorian goblets.

❷ Catleya★★
118, Av. Louis-Lepoutre
☎ 344 6364
Mon.-Sat. 10am-8pm, Sun. 10am-2pm.

It's impossible not to be drawn by the delicate leaves and rustic bouquets over-flowing from this shop onto the pavement. The florist will make up a Van Gogh or Manet bouquet for you or, if you prefer, will create one specially in an earthenware pot, which will fill your home with fragrance as it dries.

❻ Jacques Smadja★★
21, Av. Louis-Lepoutre
☎ 346 5013
Mon.-Sat. 11am-6.30pm.

A very long shop where the warmth of the East meets the coolness of steel. Here they know how to select clothes for hip and elegant men. Jacques Smadja will give you coffee and his tasteful advice, along with a wide range of classically elegant clothes and high-quality accessories from the finest sources.

❹ Graphie Sud★★★
15, Pl. Brugmann
☎ 344 3192
Tue.-Sat. 11am-6.30pm,
Sun. 11.30am-3.30pm.

Almost certainly the most beautiful and inventive display in the city. Violaine loves strange and Surrealist objects, thanksgiving plaques, structured and comfortable clothes, good chocolates, conviviality and travel. This is the perfect place to find a personalised gift such as an engraved pebble, to dress from head to toe or buy a superb piece of jewellery.

❺ Le Balmoral★★
21, Pl. Brugmann
☎ 347 0882
Tue.-Sun. 9am-7pm.

A real 1960s milk bar with pin-ups from the silver screen and an American menu. Club sandwiches, salads with a choice of four different dressings, home-made burgers, cheesecakes, brownies, cookies and all kinds of milkshakes are on the menu. Perfect for a late breakfast with pancakes,

as you can eat here any time. Children are welcome, with bibs and baby food all part of the service.

❻ Atelier B
197, Rue Berkendael
☎ 344 9564
Tue.-Sat. 11am-6pm
(ring to enter).

Viviane Behar is a talented silversmith who takes inspiration from antiquity to create unique jewellery using combinations of stones, baroque pearls, gold and silver. Fancy a new setting for an old stone, or a necklace and earrings as worn by a Roman lady? She gets you to try a model in wax before casting. And, surprisingly, it'll cost you no more than a piece of costume jewellery.

❼ Hôtel Hannon★★★
1, Av. de la Jonction
☎ 538 4220
1-6pm, closed Mon., hols and 15 July-15 Aug.
Entry charge.

Originally this building was an Art Nouveau jewel created in 1903 by J. Brunfaut for his friend E. Hannon, an engineer who was also a keen photographer. Today the great symbolist frescoe by Baudoüin in the stairwell and the mosaic floors and marbles selected by Gallé are all that remains of the past splendours of this house, which is home to the photographic organisation Contretype. Retrospectives of Hannon's photographic work are regularly held here.

Cinquantenaire
megalomania and museums

Leopold II had big ideas for celebrating his kingdom's jubilee: a triumphal arch, a park, an exhibition centre and a wide avenue. This ambitious project was opened 25 years later and helped to create a residential district favoured by the wealthy bourgeoisie, who settled here in magnificent private mansions. A century later they're now occupied by the Eurocrats who followed the bulldozers into the area. But while the shops here tend to be upmarket and unexciting, it's worth making the effort to come and visit the museums in their leafy setting.

❶ Royal Museums of Art and History★★★
10, Parc du Cinquantenaire
☎ 741 7211
Tue.-Fri. 9.30am-5pm, Sat., Sun. and hols 10am-5pm.
Entry charge.

You'll have to pick and choose from the vast collections in Belgium's largest museum, as

it contains objects from all around the world. Don't miss the great colonnade from Apameus, the *moai* from Easter Island, a magnificent Tupinamba cape of quetzal feathers, the god Chimù who Hergé used in *The Broken Ear* and the Horta room.

❷ Autoworld★★
11, Parc du Cinquantenaire
☎ 736 4165
Open every day 10am-6pm (5pm Oct.-Apr.)
Entry charge.

Under a great glass roof over 300 vehicles tell the story of the automobile from its conception to the 1950s. All countries are represented by exceptional models, including Belgian-made cars and motorbikes. Gems include King Albert I's Minerva (1910), the first Ford mobile home from 1924, Gaston Lagaffe's Citroën and J. F. Kennedy's Cadillac. Some reduced size models are on sale in the shop!

❸ Maison Cauchie★★★
5, Rue des Francs
☎ 673 1506
Tours the 1st weekend of the month 11am-6pm
Entry charge.

This old house-cum-studio of the painter Paul Cauchie, painstakingly renovated by the De Cissys, illustrates another side of Art Nouveau. Despite its Japanese-style sgraffiti, the pure lines of the façade are close to Austrian secessionism and Mackintosh in design. In the drawing room you can see more sgraffiti and original furniture.

❹ Aux Délices de Capoue★★★
36, Av. des Celtes
☎ 733 3833
Open every day, noon-10pm.

People come from far and wide to buy their home-made

ice-cream here. Of the forty flavours available, make sure you try *speculoos* and marzipan ice-cream, or a mandarin and gooseberry sorbet. You can eat in the clean, neat little tea-room, or take away.

❺ Du Vent dans les Voiles★
31, Rue Bâtonnier Braffort
☎ 735 5559
Mon.-Sat. 10.30am-7pm.

For women who hate close-fitting clothes Françoise Cloquet has selected fluid lines and colours that are great to wear in winter or summer. As well as the beautiful and expensive Chacok collection, you'll find equally attractive Indonesian batiks and Indian ensembles at more democratic prices. To round off your outfit, choose from the Indian-made costume jewellery and matching scarves.

❻ Dédale★★
Galerie Cinquantenaire
☎ 734 2255
Mon.-Sat. 10.30am-6.30pm.

It's playtime! Here you'll find the widest possible choice of brain-teasers, tarot cards, jig-saw puzzles, board games, games of strategy, everything an adult may want to play that uses their brain. You can play war games, perform magic tricks or read the cards

❼ Casting studio★★
Atelier de Moulages
10, Parc du Cinquantenaire
☎ 741 7294
Mon.-Fri. 9am-noon and 1.30-3.30pm.

Ever dreamed of having the Victory of Samothrace in your living-room? Well there's a life-size plaster copy of it in this studio hidden away in the museum basement. In the highly Surrealist atmosphere created by around 4,000 moulds, they reproduce masterpieces from the neighbouring museum as well as from Florence, Rome and Berlin. You'll have to wait two to four weeks to get one of these casts, which are not on display.

for your friends; but you won't find any electronic games here, as they're banned.

Around Saint-Boniface

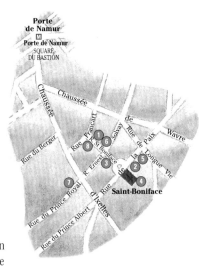

Porte de Namur
Ⓜ
Porte de Namur
SQUARE DU BASTION

Saint-Boniface

Between 'Matonge', which dances to African rhythms, and the noisy Chaussée d'Ixelles, with its shops selling cheap goods, there's a little area that's been preserved. Here every other house was designed by Ernest Blérot, an architect of the Art Nouveau movement, who was active around 1900. Coloured sgraffiti and fluid curves enliven the brick and stone façades. The atmosphere is warm and lively, generated by a young population of students from the Conservatoire and the cinema school. It's also the favourite haunt of cartoon fans, who hang around the bookshops on the Chaussée de Wavre.

❶ Comptoir Florian★★
17, Rue Saint-Boniface
☎ 513 9103
Tue.-Sat. 11am-8pm.

Proust would have loved this literary little tea-house in a shop designed by Blérot in 1900. Here you can drink rare blends or seasonal teas flavoured with green lemons and bitter oranges in summer, cinnamon and cloves in winter. There's freshly ground coffee, *pasteis* and home-made cakes, a warm welcome and a clientele of film-fans.

❷ Kasœri★★★
31, Rue de la Paix
☎ 514 2251
Mon.-Sat. 10.30am-6.30pm.

An impressive choice of dressmaking and furnishing fabrics are arranged in rolls on the shelves. The cloth is woven by artisans in India and can be used for bedspreads, a throw for your old chair or

sofa, or made into light curtains. The fibres are all natural with ethnic or unobtrusive designs and the widths vary from 110-240 cm/43-95in. A great place to visit to revamp your interior without spending a fortune.

❸ L'Ultime Atome★★
14, Rue Saint-Boniface
☎ 511 1367
**Mon.-Fri. 8.30-1am,
Sat.-Sun. and hols 10-1am.**

Don't miss the chance to stop off here for a drink or one of the tasty dishes and salads on offer at very affordable prices. Frequented by the young and not-so-young, from ice-cool types to yuppies, always full to bursting, smoky and very cosmopolitan. In the summer they put tables outside.

❹ Church of Saint-Boniface★

Built in 1847 for parishioners tired of climbing the hill after attending mass in La Cambre abbey, this is a prime example of the neo-Gothic style. Inside it's amazingly light, with pseudo-Gothic confessionals, and at the entrance on the right-hand side there's a display of faded postcards that every collector will adore.

❺ Cocoon★★★
41, Rue de la Paix
☎ 512 6486
Mon.-Sat. 10.30am-6pm.

Why not get ahead of fashion? Dominique has an exclusive range of clothes for men and women, consisting of a few designs from the next year's collection of some of fashion's top names. The result is knock-down prices, with a limited choice in any size, but a constant flow of new stock. A great place to find clothes that stand out from the crowd (extra-large sizes available) with fun accessories and helpful advice from the owner.

❻ Campion★★
11, Rue Saint-Boniface
☎ 512 1721
Tue.-Sat. 10am-1pm an d 2-6pm.

A haunt of professional photographers and demanding connoisseurs. M. Campion has a collection of cameras dating back to the early 20th century. Some of these antiques are for sale, as is a range of excellent secondhand equipment guaranteed by the shop.

❽ Yamato★
11, Rue Francart
☎ 502 2893
Tue.-Fri. noon-2pm, 7-10pm, Sat. noon-2pm, 6.30-9pm.

A little bit of Tokyo, where Japanese men in suits and ties meet fans of *gyoza* and *sake* over a bowl of soup. Sixteen seats at the bar and a bench where you can kill time trying to understand cartoons written in ideograms. Don't try lingering over your empty bowl or coming in a large party.

❼ Touijar★★
7, Rue du Prince-Royal
☎ 511 4178
Tue.-Sat. 10am-6.30pm.

Original pieces of jewellery created like sculptures, using a combination of techniques and metals. Contemporary pieces showing the influence of their designer's multiracial origins: heavy gold necklaces, broad bracelets engraved with hieroglyphs, stones in raw settings. Every piece is unique and would look fantastic with clothes by the top designers.

Rooms and restaurants

HOTELS

The new hotels are all concentrated in the business district, around the European institutions near Avenue Louise (the heart of the Art Nouveau quarter), while the old luxury hotels line the Boulevard A.-Max, apart from *Le Dixseptième* which is situated near the Grand-Place. All the others are small, comparatively modest establishments but are generally preferable to the Novtel and similar chains, which lack character and charge exorbitant prices. Those with transport will find charming hotels in an idyllic setting only 10-20 minutes from the city centre. Here comfort goes hand in hand with good prices.

CLASSIFICATION

The hotels can be split into four categories: those occupying the old, restored Belle Epoque palaces, the modern international chains, which are purely functional, the new 4 and 5-star character hotels, where the emphasis is on refinement, and, lastly, a few small, independent 2 and 3-star hotels, often converted from bourgeois residences, with a family atmosphere and varying degrees of comfort. To help ensure you have a pleasant weekend, we've decided to mention only those hotels whose atmosphere or quality of service make them stand out from the crowd, or which charge reasonable prices all year round. Although the luxury hotels do drop their prices (reductions of over 50%) at weekends (Friday and Saturday nights, sometimes Sunday), a double room (with breakfast) still comes to BF4,000-6,000. Expect to pay BF3,500 for a 3-star hotel, while the 2-star hotels charge around BF2,000-3,000 for a double room. If the hotel has a garage there's usually a charge to use it (BF800 per night), but breakfast (very generous, with different kinds of bread, cheese and cooked meats) is generally included, except in the grand hotels during the week. The 4 and 5-star hotels charge low season prices during the Christmas holidays and in July and August.

BOOKING

To book, all you have to do is phone or fax with your details and credit card number. Postal orders and eurocheques are also accepted as payment. If you don't take up your reservation, you'll be charged the price of one night's stay. The longer you book in advance, the better your chance of getting a good room (executive or luxury class) at a weekend rate in the luxury hotels, as standard rooms with poor positions are kept back for last-minute bookings. It's always a good idea to state exactly what kind of room you require (quiet, at the back or front of the building, double bed, smoking or non-smoking, etc.).Bear in mind that if you book through a travel agent, even if you aren't given a room in one of the more anonymous hotels, you're likely to end up with a very poor room in the luxury hotel of your choice since priority goes to individual clients.

Most hotels are affiliated to BTR (*Belgian Tourist Reservation*) ☎ (02) 513 7484. ✆ (02) 513 9217. This is a free booking service run by the tourist office where you'll be dealt with by an English-speaking member of staff. You'll find a brochure containing descriptions of the hotels and details of prices in every branch of the Belgian tourist information office, including those abroad.

LAST-MINUTE BOOKINGS

If you find yourself in Brussels and want a hotel room for that night or the following night, go to the TIB on Grand-Place or to the OPT (63, Rue du Marché-aux-Herbes), where the staff will find you a room free of charge if you give them an idea of your price range.

ROOMS FOR PAYING GUESTS

Try taking a room as a paying guest in someone's house. Sharing breakfast with them is a friendly way to go about your stay and gives you a different kind of insight into the real life of Brussels. You can have a room with a shared bathroom, a room with en-suite facilities or more luxurious accommodation, and prices range from BF1,250 to 3,300 for 2 people. For a list of families offering rooms, contact:

Bed & Brussels,
2, Rue Gustave Biot-1050
☎ 646 0737. ☎ 644 0114.

RESTAURANTS

To judge from the tables piled high like something out of a Brueghel painting, food has always been a major concern of the Belgians. Although the words 'Belgian cuisine' may not instantly suggest a wide range of gastronomic delights, it's no accident that the good eating guides mention several restaurants in Brussels. In practice French food comes top of the list here, but you shouldn't miss out on some of the local dishes, such as shrimp croquettes, dishes cooked in beer and all the specialities involving North Sea fish. In a cosmopolitan city like Brussels you should also take your tastebuds on a tour around the world, from Italy to Africa to Polynesia. Choosing just one out of the 1,800 eating establishments is no easy task, but always bear three golden rules in mind:
1) if a restaurant is empty at 8pm it's really not a good sign;
2) a very fashionable interior very rarely goes hand in hand with good cooking;
3) the still lifes spread out in front of the restaurants around the Grand-Place indicate that these places are tourist traps.

HOW MUCH TO PAY

Restaurants in Brussels tend to be expensive. This is due to the high cost of fresh ingredients and the high taxes. Expect to pay at least BF1,000 per person at an average restaurant. The bill rises steeply once you move into the gourmet category. However, you can always eat comparatively cheaply at one of the city's many buffet restaurants and you'll also find quite a few snack-bars serving a limited range of perfectly decent meals. Your bill will include a 15 % service charge, but it's usual to leave a small tip, particularly in the more prestigious restaurants. You'll also have to pay for valet service, which is currently very much in vogue. With a few exceptions, you should have no trouble paying your bill with your credit card.

BRUSSELS TIMING

Lunch is served between noon and 2.30pm and dinner starts at 7.30pm. You can usually order until 11pm or even midnight. Some restaurants, such as the *Falstaff*, are open round the clock, but there aren't very many of these. Most restaurants are closed at lunchtime on Saturday and on Sundays, but you'll still find good restaurants open at these times.
Brunch is becoming ever more fashionable. It generally takes the form of a full buffet at a modest price, so that people can go out to eat as a family.

HOTELS

Îlot Sacré

Amigo★★★★

1-3, Rue de l'Amigo-1000
Metro Bourse
☎ 547 4747, 🆏 513 5277.

This Renaissance building just near Grand-Place stands on the site of an old prison known as 'amigo' by the Spanish occupiers. Its comfortable rooms (some of which have a view over the city hall) and lounges decorated with old tapestries and pictures by the Dutch masters attract an upmarket clientele which includes diplomats. It also has an underground carpark, which is a great boon in this area.

Le Dixseptième
★★★★

25, Rue de la Madeleine-1000
Metro Gare Centrale
☎ 502 5744, 🆏 502 6424.

The monumental Louis XVI staircase and salons decorated with frescoes have been preserved in this lovely gabled house which was the residence of the Spanish ambasssador in the early 18th century. Every room has its own character: from the very large rooms with fireplaces, parquet flooring and chiné furnishings, to attic rooms with exposed beams and rustic furniture, to the more modern studios looking out over a leafy patio. Refined, quality service, with an excellent breakfast.

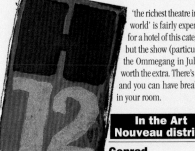

La Madeleine
★★

22, Rue de la Montagne-1000
Metro Gare Centrale
☎ 513 2973, 🆏 502 1350.

This 17th-century residence suffered a rather extreme form of renovation, which preserved nothing but the façade, behind which you'll find 52 comfortable but small rooms (apart from the larger, executive suites). It does, however, have the advantage of being one of the good affordable hotels close to Grand-Place.

Hôtel Saint-Michel★★

15, Grand-Place-1000
Metro Bourse
☎ 511 0956, 🆏 511 4600.

This is a very small hotel in the prestigious buildings of the house of the Dukes of Brabant. It has recently been renovated and some of the rooms have windows looking onto Grand-Place. A box overlooking 'the richest theatre in the world' is fairly expensive for a hotel of this category, but the show (particularly the Ommegang in July) is worth the extra. There's a lift and you can have breakfast in your room.

In the Art Nouveau district

Conrad International Brussels★★★★★

71, Av. Louise-1050
Metro Louise
☎ 542 4242, 🆏 542 4200.

This prestigious and expensive hotel occupies several 19th-century houses. It would be nice to find a more friendly atmosphere and a less Americanised decor behind its palatial façade. Even without staying in the same suite as Bill Clinton, the prices of both rooms and restaurant are too high, weekend rate included.

Manos★★★

100-104, Chaussée de Charleroi-1060
Trams 91-92-Faider
☎ 537 9682, 🆏 539 3655.

In the heart of the Art Nouveau district, a lovely old-style hotel full of oriental carpets, crystal chandeliers, gilding and marble.

Its major advantage, apart from the pleasant rooms, is an enormous garden where chickens lay the eggs for breakfast, which is served outside on fine days.

Rembrandt★★

42, Rue de la Concorde-1050
Metro Louise
☎ 512 7139, 𝔽 511 7136.

A stone's throw from the smart shops of Avenue Louise, this building is on the corner of a quiet street and has 13 light-filled rooms. Very well kept, with a lovely smell of wax, this is an ideal family hotel for those who set store by the welcome they receive. Depending on your budget, you can either have a suite in the attic (no. 15), the very pleasant no. 6 with its little lounge, or one of the more modest rooms.

Les Bluets★★

124, Rue Berckmans-1060
Metro Hôtel des Monnaies

☎ 534 3983, 𝔽 543 0970.

As long as you don't smoke or party all night, you'll be made very welcome in this small, family-run hotel with its 11 personalised rooms. Marble fireplaces, painted ceilings, crocheted curtains, old furniture, ornaments and lots of flowers on the veranda, where you can have breakfast in the company of

statues of the Virgin Mary and a few exotic birds. From the very large (no. 2) to the smaller and prettier (nos 3, 10), the rooms are all reasonably priced. No lift.

Welcome★★

5, Rue du Peuplier-1000
Metro Sainte-Catherine
☎ 219 9546, 𝔽 217 1887.

In the little preservation area of the former Béguinage, this small hotel, with just six rooms, is big on comfort and flowery decor. Exemplary welcome and service, peace and quiet guaranteed and free parking. It's excellent value and in an interesting area with the best fish restaurants in town.

Hôtel Atlas★★★★

30, Rue du Vieux-Marché-aux-Grains-1000
Metro Bourse
☎ 502 6006, 𝔽 502 6935.

The lovely stone façade hides 88 well-appointed rooms that are surprisingly quiet for this trendy area, with a view over either the courtyard or the shady square. The decor is sober in basic

colours and the family welcoming. A double surprise awaits you in the breakfast room: a generous and varied buffet and part of the 11th-century city wall. Excellent value for money.

Métropole★★★★★

31, Pl. de Brouckère-1000
Metro De Brouckère
☎ 217 2300, 𝔽 218 0220.

Sacha Guitry's favourite hotel. This most magnificent of the Belle Époque grand hotels, with a profusion Numidia marble, gilded bronze and columns, has just celebrated its centenary. Sample both the acclaimed cuisine of Dominique Michou accompanied by the wine you have brought with you (Wednesdays only) and the thalassotherapy centre. On the other hand the rooms vary greatly in quality, with the ones at the front

being the brightest. You're most likely to get a good room at the weekend rate in summer.

Le Plaza★★★★

118-126, Bd A.-Max-1000
Metro Rogier
☎ 227 6700, 𝔽 227 6720.

A grand hotel dating from 1930 designed by Michel Polak. Admirably restored in 1996, it has 193 rooms, including some suites, in which the discreet luxury of the delicate fabrics and period woodwork combine

harmoniously with the modern bathrooms. Excluding Winston Churchill, the most notable guests have generally been great names from the music-hall and French cinema – including Simone Signoret and Louis Jouvet. The restaurant has a *trompe l'œil* dome and other attractions include an old cinema, amethyst crystal chandeliers and an authentic Gobelin tapestry. Garage parking is available for a supplementary charge.

Crowne Plaza★★★★

3, Rue Gineste-1210
Metro Rogier
☎ 203 6200, 🅕 203 5555.

Built in 1910 in a very modernist style by A. Pompe, this hotel has witnessed many different stylistic currents of the 20th century: Art Deco after World War II, the new look for Expo' 58 and renovation in 1982 after a narrow escape from the property developers. The period furniture unearthed in the cellars has been put back into the rooms, giving them an added touch of originality. Ask for room 651, a jewel of Art Nouveau with inlaid woodwork, or a room overlooking the park. If you have the means, you can always have the suite where Grace Kelly stayed in 1956.

Botanique

Astoria★★★★★

103, Rue Royale-1000
Metro Botanique
☎ 227 0505, 🅕 217 1150.

A monumental entrance lined with granite columns, a gilded neo-Victorian hall lit by thousands of lights, a majestic staircase and a restaurant with an excellent reputation. This grand hotel from the Belle Époque, where young emperor Hirohito of Japan stayed in 1921, has lost none of its splendour. You can have a drink in its Orient Express-styled bar, listen to one of the Sunday concerts, stay in the most luxurious of suites or in a room that's less expensive but just as comfortable. Best are rooms 117, 126, 127 or 129.

Hôtel du Congrès★★

42-44, Rue du Congrès-1000
Metro Madou
☎ 217 18 90, 🅕 217 18 97.

This hotel, in a quiet area, has the comfortable atmosphere of two private houses and the 53 rooms, which may lack character, all have a shower, WC and television. To get your day off to a good start, breakfast includes Viennese pastries, cereals, fruit and Belgian speciality breads. The carpark has 7 places, you'll get a good welcome and there's a promotional rate at weekends. Booking advisable.

Sabina★

78, Rue du Nord-1000
Metro Madou
☎ 218 2637, 🅕 219 3239.

A 19th-century bourgeois house with wood panelling and mouldings, offering 24 light, quiet rooms with all mod. cons, including television. Modest prices and a friendly welcome.

Cinquantenaire

Stanhope★★★★★
9, Rue du Commerce-1000
Metro Trône
☎ 506 9111, ℻ 512 1708.

This hotel in the 'European'

area is a high spot of English-style refinement with 50 light, very comfortable rooms. The penthouse at the end of the garden is ideal for a romantic (if pricey) weekend. Personalised service, garage parking for an extra charge and an excellent restaurant, which sadly is closed on Saturdays and Sundays.

Montgoméry
★★★★★

134, Av. de Tervueren-1150
Metro Montgoméry
☎ 741 8511,
℻ 741 8500.

The recent façade hides all the comfort of an old English stately home. The spacious rooms come with a choice of three atmospheres: cottagey, British with a flowery dash of Vichy France,

or colonial. Lovely and cosy, there's a library with a log fire, interesting books and deep sofas where generous breakfasts are served at weekends. Other attractions include a garage and weekend rates (the 3rd night from Saturday to Sunday is free).

Armorial★★
101, Bd Brand Whitlock-1200
Metro Georges Henri
☎ 734 5636, ℻ 734 5005.

A cosy house with well-polished parquet floors and period furniture in the 15 rooms, which are all different sizes and levels of comfort. For peace and quiet ask for a view over the courtyard, but the larger rooms (1-4) are at the front. A lift and breakfast are provided; for dinner there are a few good Chinese restaurants in the area.

In surrounding areas

Les Tourelles★★★
135, Av. Winston-Churchill-1180
Bus 60-Cavell
☎ 344 0284, ℻ 346 4270.

Not far from La Cambre wood, in a very peaceful district, this delightful manor house with a magnolia tree outside was, until 1934, a boarding school for young ladies of good families. It has retained this rather outdated character in its lounges and in its 22 rooms, not all of which are equipped with a bathroom. Ask for a room on the first floor with a balcony overlooking the courtyard. It's better to book in advance, particularly when there's a tournament at the neighbouring Léo tennis club.

Le Manoir du Lac★★★★
4, Av. Hoover-1332 Genval
☎ 655 6311, ℻ 655 6455.

Twenty minutes by car from Brussels and 5 minutes from Genval station, a flowery cottage nestling in a garden full of rare plants. Very romantic with its English-style lounge and terrace, where you can breakfast in the sun. It also has a sauna and a Turkish bath for real relaxation. Lots to see and do in the local area (Lake Genval) either on foot or by bicycle. Very good prices at weekends.

You'll have to book well in advance if you want to get a table in this Art Nouveau centre of gourmet eating. Chef Pierre Wynants explores all the flavours of classic French cuisine with a few additions from the East. His vegetable mousses are real masterpieces. For a cheaper option, there's a set menu of four dishes for BF1,975. Smart dress only.

RESTAURANTS

Îlot Sacré

Aux Armes de Bruxelles★★★

13, Rue des Bouchers-1000
Metro Bourse
☎ 511 5550
Noon-11pm, closed Mon. and 15 June-15 July.

A Brussels institution serving authentic local cuisine, mainly poultry and North Sea fish, as well as beef *carbonade* with gueuze beer or Brussels *potée* or boiled meat with cabbage. Make sure you sample the lobster *waterzoi* and Zeeland mussels. A speciality meal washed down with muscadet costs BF1,695.

De l'Ogenblik★★★

1, Gal. des Princes-1000
Metro Bourse
☎ 511 61 51
Lunchtimes and eves, closed Sun. and hols at lunchtime.

This restaurant on the corner of Galerie Saint-Hubert is one of the most highly rated in the area

and is frequented by artists. Delicious French cuisine with a menu that changes every day according to available ingredients, with a few reliable dishes, such as salmon mille-feuilles, lobster and crayfish tails and grilled calf's sweetbreads. It's a bit expensive, but well worth the price.

La Taverne du Passage★★★

30, Gal. de la Reine-1000
Metro Gare Centrale
☎ 512 3731
Open every day noon-midnight, closed Wed and Thu. in June and July.

No one can claim to know Brussels until they've visited this venerable Art Deco brasserie and sampled the sublime shrimp croquettes. Some good wines and delicious Belgian and French specialities, but sadly the service has gone downhill in recent times.

Bourse

Comme chez Soi★★★★★

23, Pl. Rouppe-1000
Metro Anneessens
☎ 512 2921
Lunchtime and evenings, closed Sun. and Mon., in July and Christmas holidays.

In't Spinnekopke★★

1, Pl. du Jardin-aux-Fleurs-1000
Metro Sainte-Catherine
☎ 511 8695
Open every day lunchtimes and evenings except Sat. lunchtime, Sun. and hols.

The coach no longer stops outside this 1762 inn, but inside they still speak *Brusseleir* and serve dependably good local dishes. If you like beer, so much the better, as there's plenty around in both the drinking glasses and cooking pots, from the *carbonades* with *lambic* to the fillet steak with gueuze beer and guinea foul with raspberry beer. It's also one of the few places where you can drink *faro*.

Le Petit Boxeur★★

3, Rue Borgval-1000
☎ 511 4000
Open evenings, closed Sun. and Mon. Booking advisable at weekends.

Walls with a dark brown veneer, big mirrors, chandeliers and beautiful tables covered in cotton damask, crystal and silverware: the ambiance is pure Frank Sweijd. This aesthete and gourmet constantly reinvents the simplest dishes, giving every flavour a hint of the sublime. The menu changes with the seasons, with surprises such as squid lasagne and vegetarian *tartare* and a fine wine list of Bordeaux and Burgundies.

L'Étoile d'Or★★

30, Rue des Foulons-1000
Tram Anneessens
☎ 502 6048
Lunchtimes and evenings, closed Sat. lunchtime and Sun. and 15 July-15 Aug.

One of the last real Brussels *caberdouches* with a cast iron stove in the middle of the room and a lovely old floor, which has earned it the nickname

rotte planchei ('rotten floor'). On the blackboard you'll find Belgian specialities (finely sliced poultry with chicory, *waterzoi*, *entrecôte au lambic*, and Brussels cheese) and Spanish or French dishes, depending on what the chef feels like making that day.

Marolles

L'Idiot du Village★★★★

19, Rue Notre-Seigneur-1000
Bus 48-Chapelle
☎ 502 5582
Lunchtimes and evenings, closed Sat., Sun., 15 July-15 Aug. and 24 Dec.-2 Jan.

A place where you can explore beauty and flavour. Step through the velvet curtains into a dazzling, theatrical atmosphere and enjoy a very warm welcome. At a candlelit table you can sample delicious local dishes reinvented by the French chef, such as raw salmon *tartare* or scallops and foie gras. It's trendy, quite expensive, with a high class clientele (a favourite of King Albert and Queen Paola). Book well in advance.

Les Larmes du Tigre★★★

21, Rue de Wynants-1000
Metro Louise
☎ 512 1877
Lunchtimes and evenings, closed Sat. lunchtime.

A real festival of Thai flavours in

a subtle, exotic restaurant situated behind the law courts. They serve a little sorbet between courses to aid digestion and the staff never stop smiling. Don't miss the buffet, particularly on Sunday evenings, when you have a wonderful choice for a very affordable price.

Sainte-Catherine

La Belle Maraîchère★★★

11a, Pl. Sainte-Catherine-1000
Metro Sainte-Catherine
☎ 512 9759
Lunchtimes and evenings., closed Wed. and Thu.

Simply the best fish restaurant in the area.

Chez Henri★★★

**113, Rue de Flandre-1000
Metro Sainte-Catherine
☎ 219 6415
Every day, lunchtimes and
evenings.**

You eat your mussels from the
pot on paper tablecloths in this
restaurant that smells of fried
food. There's lobster with chips
and caviar imported directly
from Iran. The ingredients are
fresh and the locals love it, but
the prices are over the top.

Le Vistro★★

**16, Quai aux Briques-1000
Metro Sainte-Catherine
☎ 512 4181
Lunchtimes and evenings,
closed Sat. lunch and Sun.**

With bistrot-style seats and the
day's menu written up on the
blackboard, this friendly little
restaurant, serves mainly seafood, including surprising
creations such as fish black
pudding. You can also have
ultra-fresh lobster, oysters, mussels and home-made desserts –
only the shrimp croquettes aren't
that great. Reasonably priced.

Sablon

Vert de Gris★★

**63, Rue des Alexiens-1000
Bus 48-Chapelle
☎ 514 2168
Tue.-Fri. lunchtimes and
evenings, closed Sat. and
Sun. lunchtime.**

The extraordinary interior is part
Mediterranean grocer's shop,
part Baroque dining-room and
part colonial smoking-room
with a theatrical garden terrace.
With all this you'd expect to find
a rather more inventive menu
than the eternal scampi and
pasta dishes. That said, you can
eat better and more cheaply here
than in many other places.

Saint-Boniface and Place Flagey

Dolma★★

**329, Chaussée d'Ixelles-1050
Bus 71-Flagey
☎ 649 8981
Mon.-Sat. noon-midnight
and 7am-9.30pm.**

If you like vegetables and
Tibetan cuisine, this restaurant
is not to be missed. Beneath the
roof of a nomad's tent there's
a wonderful buffet, lunchtimes
and evenings. A real feast for
BF390 (full meal) in a Buddhist-
style environment. One evening
a month there's a concert of
world music. Also take a visit to
the shop next door – it's a gold-
mine of organic and macrobio-
tic delights.

Notos★★

**24, Rue Solvay-1050
Metro Porte de Namur
☎ 513 2959
Lunchtimes and evenings,
closed Sun. and Mon.
Booking essential in the
evening.**

You'll find all the exquisite tastes
of the Mediterranean in this

little local restaurant where they
serve delicious dishes cooked
with olive oil that are simple but
full of flavour. Kebabs with
yoghurt, aubergine caviar,
artichokes with lemon, roast
peppers and seafood, all prepared to old family recipes. And
you'll always find a very friendly
welcome.

Trente Rue de la Paille★★★★

**30, Rue de la Paille-1000
Bus 48-Grand-Sablon
☎ 512 0715
Mon.-Fri. lunchtimes and
evenings.**

The menu combines tasty fish
and meat specialities. Highly
imaginative, subtly flavoured
dishes by chef André Martini. The
list of French wines is also up to
scratch with around a hundred
bottles. Why not treat yourself to
lunch – 3 courses at BF1,250.

De Brouckère

Roma★★★★

12-14, Rue des Princes-1000
Metro La Monnaie
☎ 218 3430
Lunchtimes and evenings
(until 1am on performance
nights), closed Sat.
lunchtime and Sun.

A classy interior next to the Théâtre de la Monnaie with Italian cuisine to match. Besides the *à la carte* menu and set meal at BF1,350, there are dishes of the day according to availability, with an excellent choice of tastily prepared fish. Of the pasta specialities, try the sublime *agnolotti* (ravioli with cheese). All in all, excellent gourmet Italian cuisine accompanied by good Italian wines.

Around Cinquantenaire Saint Gilles

Inada★★★★

73, Rue de la Source-1060
Metro Louise
☎ 538 0113
Lunchtimes and evenings,
closed Sat. lunch, Sun., Mon.
and last two weeks of July.

A very fine Japanese chef assisted by probably the best wine steward in Brussels serving French cuisine enhanced with subtle, Asiatic flavours. A real feast that you won't forget in too much of a hurry.

En face de Parachute★★★

578, Chaussée de Waterloo-1050
Bus 38-Bascule
☎ 346 4741
Lunchtimes and evenings,
closed Sun. and Mon.
No credit cards. Booking
essential in the evening.

This restaurant is packed with a trendy crowd who come to sample the dishes of the week created by Nounou. A great connoisseur of Bordeaux if the wine list is anything to go by, there are many other treasures in his well-stocked cellar of 350 wines. The cuisine is somewhere between French and Italian, with the chef's own inventive touch. A relaxed bistrot atmosphere and lunchtime dish of the day for BF280.

Rosticceria Fiorentina★★

45, Rue Archimède-1000
Metro Schuman
☎ 734 9236
Lunchtimes and evenings,
closed Sat.

Good home cooking from chef Lucca in an unpretentious setting. Minestrone, pasta dishes, roast veal with *faggioli* and *fegato*. In winter there's plenty of game. Dish of the day is BF400, served with Tuscan wine of course. A fine restaurant that hasn't yet been taken over by the Eurocrats, who prefer a bit more luxury.

Uccle

Le Pain et Le Vin★★★

812a, Chaussée
d'Alsemberg-1180
Tram 55-Ritweger
☎ 332 3774
Lunchtime and evenings,
closed Sat. lunch and Sun.

Good food and drink are the watchwords of the chef and talented wine steward, who've chosen a beautiful, tastefully decorated building to practice their arts. Subtle flavours draw on both French and Italian cuisine while the humour is very Belgian. Accompany your meal with a choice from the unusually adventurous list of 200 wines. There's also a lovely shady garden and lunch at BF395.

For the decor

La Cité du Dragon★★★★

1022-1024, Chaussée de Waterloo-1180
☎ 375 8080
Open every day lunchtime and eve.

Worth seeing for the garden alone, with its exotic plants, waterfalls and half-moon bridge. In the equally refined interior of rosewood and antiques, you can sample authentic Peking, Szechuan or Cantonese cuisine. Besides the traditional dishes of suckling pig and duck, served in 3 or 4 courses (skin, meat, soup) which must be ordered in advance, you'll find an extraordinarily wide selection of different menus, from BF690-2,350. In winter the buffet brunch provides a relatively inexpensive chance to sample all the dishes

Pasta Commedia★★★★

3, Av. J.-et- P.-Carsoel-1180
Bus 43-Place Saint-Job
☎ 372 0607
Open every day lunchtimes and evenings.

Very successful thanks to the happy marriage of a grandiose interior with Antonio Pinto's talents as a chef. In the open kitchen, dominated by a stage framed with heavy, dark red curtains, he creates extraordinary Italian dishes such as lobster ravioli on a bed of wild mushrooms, caramelised roast saddle of hare with quince, mallard duck with marsala, as well as home-made pasta. There are also some exceptional wines on the list, again exclusively Italian.

La Grande Écluse★★★

77, Bd Poincaré-1070
Metro Midi
☎ 522 3025
Lunchtimes and evenings, closed Sat. and Sun. lunch.

A most unusual interior full of the pipes, metal girders and machinery of a former lock. This recently opened restaurant is all the rage and has the great merit of highlighting Brussels' forgotten industrial past. Decent food with a great many dishes

using fresh ingredients, unforgettable desserts (the chef trained at Wittamer's!), a vegetarian menu and generous portions, but the wines are a little expensive. Valet-parking and a garden terrace.

Les Bacchanales★★

62, Chaussée de Louvain-1210
Metro Madou.
☎ 218 1444
Lunchtimes and evenings (until 1am), closed Mon. and Tue. evenings and Sun.

Aldo Gigli, a designer of ephemeral cinema sets, has transformed a long, high corridor into a restaurant on two floors, whose *trompe l'œil* decor is somewhat bizarre with its astounding cocktail of constructions made from marble and shards of china combined with twisted ironwork. Plenty to explore on the food side too, such as white pudding with calf's sweetbreads and morel mushrooms, but the bill can be fairly hefty.

A real Italian bistrot where you can have a coffee, grab a *bruschetta* or try the pasta dish of the day.

Le Pain Quotidien

16, Rue A. Dansaert-1000
Metro Bourse
☎ 502 2361
Open every day 7.30am-7.30pm.

A large table of pale wood, fashionable varnished walls, a few pots of dried tomatoes and home-made preserves. The successful concept of eating good sandwiches in trendy company has spread and new branches have opened all over Brussels.

Osteria A l'Ombra

2, Rue des Harengs-1000
Metro Bourse
☎ 511 6710
10am-midnight, closed Sun.

A Venetian-style *osteria* housed in an early 20th-century former fish-shop a stone's throw from Grand-Place, where you can have breakfast in the morning or eat *bruschetta, tramezzini, antipasti* and *crostini* all day long, washed down with a Prosecco.

LIGHT MEALS AND SNACKS

Passiflore

97, Rue du Bailli-1050
Bus 54-Trinité
☎ 538 4210
Open every day 8am-7pm.

The interior of this café opposite

the Baroque church is decorated yellow and blue, with ottoman seats and china tables. It's frequented as much by men as women, who come for a bite of something savoury or sweet and a cappucino or fresh fruit juice.

Intermezzo

16, Rue des Princes-1000
Metro De Brouckère
☎ 218 0311
Mon.-Sat. 12-3pm and Fri. 7-10pm.

Tapas Locas

74, Rue du Marché-au-Charbon-1000
Metro Bourse
☎ 502 1268
Open every day 7pm-1am.

Enjoy a gargantuan meal of different *tapas* or savour a dish of octopus with sweet peppers.

Tea for Two

394, Chaussée de Waterloo-1060
Trams 91-92-Ma-Campagne
☎ 538 3896
Tue.-Sun. 11am-7pm.

The main room is very English in style, with two more intimate little rooms, one decorated in blue, the other gilded, where you can drink smoked Chinese tea or try wonderful brews flavoured with lotus flowers, essence of mandarin or rose petals. Scones, delicious cheesecake and English cakes are available for afternoon tea or Sunday brunch.

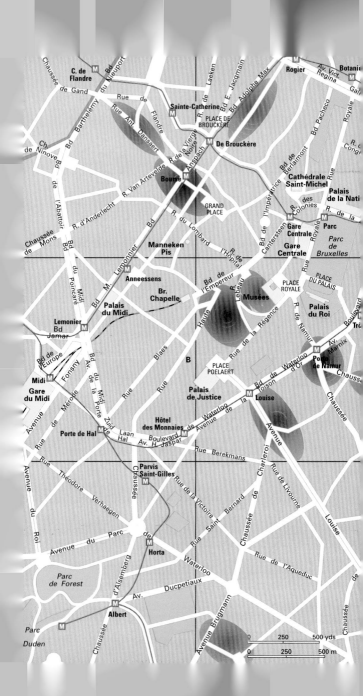

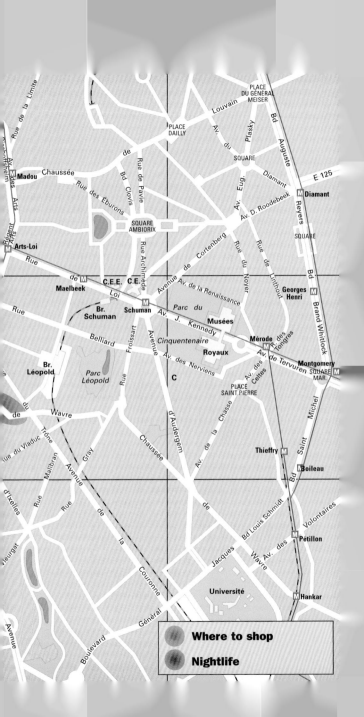

Where to shop

Nightlife

Shopping Practicalities

OPENING TIMES

Shops in Brussels are open 10am-6.30pm Tuesday to Saturday. On Mondays they're generally closed, though some small shops open at 1.30pm. Remember some shops still close for lunch between 12.30 and 1.30pm. These days, more and more shops are opening on Sundays, especially in the tourist areas, Îlot Sacré, Sablon, Marolles and around Place Brugmann. You should also remember that Sunday is the sacred 'junk shop day'. The TIB and daily papers can provide you with information about other hunting-grounds besides the markets on Place du Jeu-de-Balle and in Sablon.

HOW TO PAY

The vast majority of shops will accept credit cards for purchases over BF1,000, particularly Visa, Diner's Club, American Express and Eurocard. For other cards you're best advised to check the stickers on the door before you go inside. A signature is enough to secure your purchase. Eurocheques and travellers cheques are accepted everywhere. However, it's always better to use an automatic cash machine to withdraw money in Belgian francs directly from your own account than to pay in any kind of foreign currency.

Whenever you buy something, make sure you ask for a receipt. You may be required to show it at customs and it will also be useful should you ever want to sell the item you've just bought or if you need to fill out an insurance claim form following a burglary.

HOW MUCH TO PAY

Retailers are legally obliged to display the price of every item they have on sale. The only exceptions to this are dealers in bric-a-brac and antiques, which means that you may be able to bargain in these shops.

SALES

Sales run for a full month twice a year, starting on 1 January and 1 July. To find out about special offers and discount sales (shop closures and ends of lines), buy a paper called *Vlan*. Remember you won't be able to obtain a refund for sale items or exchange them.

DEPARTMENT STORES

Three stores called Innovation, Bon Marché and Grand Bazar have now all become part of the same group with the highly unimaginative name of GB-INNO-BM, which now has only one large store on Rue Neuve. These days, the Belgians go in for shopping centres (such as City 2 and the Woluwé Shopping Center), where you'll find retailers selling everything from food to household electrical items, and covered malls (to keep out the weather), which tend to be colonised by shops selling expensive clothes. The best-known malls (Toison d'Or, Porte Louise and Espace Louise) are now in decline as the boutiques migrate towards more fashionable locations, such as Boulevard de Waterloo and Avenue Louise.

WHERE TO BUY

No-one goes to the Avenue de la Toison-d'Or any more. If you want to find the smart shops, you have to cross the road to Boulevard de Waterloo and walk down Avenue Louise. Halfway along, you'll find Rue A. Dansaert, which is now the centre of trendy fashion in Brussels. And since Armani moved into Sablon, it looks as though the antique shops here will all soon be replaced by designer outlets.

DELIVERY

If you want to have an item you've bought sent back home, the shop may well be able to provide you with the name of a reputable transportation company. If they can't, you'll have to decide whether you want to send your goods by air, which is quick but expensive, or surface mail, which will take longer but which offers you greater flexibility where price is concerned. An insurance premium is automatically included in the transportation price quoted. If you want to have a really valuable item delivered, you should find a specialist company:

MOCLA EXPRESS
☎ 268 0561.
A company specialising in transporting artworks by land, air and sea.

BATAC
☎ 425 3246.
Speedy delivery, insurance premium in proportion to the price of the item being transported, individualised packaging, competitive prices.

MAERTENS
☎ 751 8191. Door-to-door delivery and storage of artworks.

CUSTOMS FORMALITIES

There are no customs formalities for EU citizens, provided they can show a receipt proving that duty was paid on the purchase in Belgium. No specific regulations apply to antiques, as long as you show a certificate of authenticity and a bill made out by the seller. If you're caught in possession of forged documents the goods will be confiscated and you'll have to pay a heavy fine. You may also be charged with receiving stolen goods when you get back home.

Those not resident in the EU may be able to get a reimbursment of VAT on larger purchases. To do this ask the vendor for a special form, which you'll have to fill in at the border.

FINDING YOUR WAY

Next to each address in the Shopping and Nightlife sections, you'll find its location indicated on the map of Brussels on pages 76–77.

BELGIAN DESIGNERS

Take advantage of your visit to Brussels to explore the latest creations by Belgian designers, some of whom have now acquired international status. Whether you are looking for chic, timeless, classic or seriously avant-garde, you'll discover there's something for everyone in Belgian fashion, and at very affordable prices too.

Olivier Strelli
72, Av. Louise (B2/3)
Tram 92-Stéphanie
☎ **512 5607**
Mon.-Sat. 10am-6.30pm.

His preferred colours are turquoise blue and dark red, his favourite fabric is linen. A degree of continuity in the cut means that you can combine elements from the new collections with clothes from the season before. The transparent moiré-effect blazer can be either worn over jeans or a long dress, and the classic tailored jacket can be swapped for a long, low-cut tunic.

There's plenty here for the men too, including perfectly cut jackets and waistcoats in wonderfully vibrant colours.

Natan
158, Av. Louise (B2/3)
Tram 94-Defacqz
☎ **647 1001**
Mon.-Sat. 10am-6pm.

The window display is minimalist, the prices (which aren't displayed) are not. To enter this magnificent former mansion, you have to display your worthiness and your designer accessories, otherwise you'll be shown the door.

If you're a fan of black, grey and natural tones, sober lines and well-cut suits, spangled tops and sheath dresses, you should either wait for the sales or start saving now.

Stijl
74, Rue A.- Dansaert (A1)
Bus 63-Dansaert
☎ **512 0313**
Mon.-Sat. 10.30am-6.30pm.

Showcase for the big-name Flemish designers including Dries Van Noten, Dirk Bikkembergs and Ann Demeulemeester.

Kaat Tilley
4, Gal. du Roi (B1)
Metro Gare Centrale
☎ **514 0763**
Mon.-Fri. 10am-6.30pm and Sat. 10.30am-6.30pm.

If you're less than 1.80m/5ft 11in tall and well-endowed in the bust department, don't even think of trying on the creations of this

Flemish designer. In the shop's studiedly scruffy interior fabrics are draped and laced, skirts flare out, straps are the thinnest of the thin and knits are loose. Transparent or stretchy materials are combined to create a long-line silhouette. Once inside do take a look at the extraordinary 'bridal gown' department and (trickier this...) try to make the sales assistant smile.

Nicole Cadine

28, Rue A.- Dansaert (A1)
Metro Bourse
☎ 503 4826
Mon.-Sat. 10am-6.30pm.

Inside this grey interior with its heavy moiré hangings you'll find a display of the many creations of this Antwerp-trained designer. She favours plain, natural fibres in textures ranging from simple weaves to intricate crochets with the accent on layers of light, comfortable clothing. A vast choice of dresses for day or evening wear (BF3,000-BF5,000), cotton voile tunics, flowing trousers, hats, scarves (BF1,500) and blouses. Very hard to leave empty-handed.

Chine

2, Rue Van Artevelde (A1)
Metro Bourse
☎ 503 1499
Mon.-Sat. 11am-6.30pm.

Guillaume Thys has a passion for silk and his collections are based on influences from China where his favourite material was discovered. His silk comes in every form: woven, knitted, crocheted, pleated, moiré, embroidered or beaded, and he also uses voile, jersey, crêpe and taffeta. Elegant, fluid clothes to please any woman from the youngest to the more mature (BF8,000-10,000 for a dress; blouses at BF3,500). A range of jeans adds the finishing touch to the classy ensembles.

Isabelle Baines

48, Rue du Pépin (B2)
Metro Louise
☎ 502 1373
Tue.-Sat. 10.30am-6.30pm,
Mon. 2-6.30pm.

Isabelle Baines has a reputation for making perfectly shaped knitted jumpers of excellent quality. What's more, she makes knitwear for the whole family from the age of two upwards. So you'll be able to borrow your husband's cardigan or wear a jumper to match your daughter's. The winter knitwear is all hand-made and therefore a bit more expensive (BF7,950). Expect to pay around BF6,500 for a cotton cardigan; BF4,950 for a short-sleeved jumper. An investment you'll never regret.

Elvis Pompilio

18, Rue du Lombard (A1)
Bus 48-Plattesteen
☎ 511 1188
Mon.-Sat. 10.30am-6.30pm.

Elvis's hats are like the man himself: fantastical, colourful and surprising. The aim was to bring hats back into fashion and the trick was to invent a flexible hat whose look can be changed in an instant from classic to sporty or smart. For winter styles hare-skin or fake fur is added to the felt, while straw tops the bill in

summer. But the crested woollen cap and cowboy hat also have their devotees. From BF2,500 for a cap to BF15,000 for a sophisticated hat, there's something for everyone, from the penniless student to the well-heeled woman-about-town.

WOMEN'S FASHIONS

High fashion isn't only French or Italian. In Brussels' shops you'll find everything: elegance, timelessness, unique items and designer creations, clothes that are trendy, sensible or just downright extravagant. Something for every woman between the ages of 12 and 70, whatever their budget. And some shops now open on Sundays, too.

Rue Blanche

35-41, Rue A.-Dansaert (A1)
Metro Bourse
☎ **512 0314**
Mon.-Sat. 11am-6.30pm.

Quiet colours and elegant, impeccably cut clothes to flatter the shape of your body. From the very formal to sportswear, all kinds of combinations are possible since you can dress from head to toe in the Rue Blanche brand, even down to the hat and eau de toilette.

Prototype

13, Rue du Pont-de-la-Carpe (A1)
Metro Bourse
☎ **511 6143**
Mon.-Sat. 11am-6.30pm.

Striped or plain, with or without a zip, in cotton, wool or jersey, here you'll find the timeless basics that your boyfriend will be bound to borrow, if it isn't the other way round. Not for the over 30s.

Danaqué

2, Gal. des Princes (B1)
Metro Gare Centrale
☎ **511 3533**
Mon.-Sat. 11am-6.30pm.

In this elegant shop with its interior of wood and wrought iron, you'll find clothes at very affordable prices made of natural fabrics in carmine, sienna, indigo, brick red and natural shades. Ample dresses to wear with a scarf, kimono jackets, lace blouses and unusual jumpers, there are fashions here to suit every age for women who like full, flowing outfits.

Mariella Burani

29, Rue de Namur (B2)
Metro Porte de Namur
☎ **514 0885**
Mon.-Sat. 10.30am-6.30pm.

Extremely feminine Italian fashions, well-finished and made in fabrics that are comfortable to wear. Combinations of printed designs, reversible jackets and dresses, short or long lines, fur-lined coats, chiffons, all with the same freshness and fluidity winter or summer. Of course these qualities aren't cheap: BF15,000 for a dress; BF7,000 for a pair of trousers.

César et Rosalie

50, Rue de Rollebeek (B2)
Bus 48-Grand-Sablon
☎ 514 5864
Mon.-Sat. 10.30am-6.30pm, Sun. 11am-3pm.

The same designs of comfortable clothes in different colours and fabrics depending on the season. Good, basic items and baggy jumpers you can jazz up with accessories such as a velvet scarf or some new jewellery.

La Belle et la Bête

73, Rue A.-Dansaert (A1)
Metro Bourse
☎ 502 6616
Mon.-Sat. 11am-7pm.

This is the place to find smart clothes with a little touch of originality. They are well-cut from good quality material and the colours are quietly sensible, as are the flowery-prints of the dresses, blouses and scarves. You won't have to wait for the sales to afford the clothes either as the prices are very reasonable (suit BF7,500; knitted top BF2,800).

Moi et Moi

13, Gal. Louise (B2)
Metro Louise
☎ 511 2134
Mon.-Sat. 10am-7pm.

At Strelli's junior collection you will find the same bright colours (yellow, apple-green, turquoise and orange), but here they are more daring and provocative designs for young women. Crumpled skirts, straight-cut dresses, formal jackets and beautiful knitwear, all very contemporary clothes at affordable prices (about 40% cheaper than at the Strelli shop). It's here that you'll also find the rather specialised collections from Article, Moment par Moment, and Toi mon Toi.

Côté Maille

52, Rue du Bailli (B3)
Bus 54-Lesbroussart
☎ 649 9008
Tue.-Sat. 10.30am-6.30pm.

The jumpers, dresses, trousers, jackets and T-shirts are imported directly from Italy, France and England, which explains the competitive prices for good-quality clothing.

The stock is continually updated and follows all the latest fashion trends with exclusive items such as velvet by Daisy Kuits. Cotton jackets at BF1,700; cotton jumpers at BF1,400.

Point-Virgule

14, Rue des Fripiers (B1)
Metro De Brouckère
☎ 219 0756
Mon.-Sat. 10am-6.30pm.

This is a Belgian label which specialises exclusively in knitwear for women in their 30s and 40s. Here you'll find trendy colours and figure-hugging clothes to co-ordinate with cotton voile tunics and knitwear. A wide range of designs, from T-shirts to dresses – though no jackets – all at very affordable prices. Dresses from BF2,100; trousers at BF2,800.

Patrick Pitschon

80, Rue A.-Dansaert (A1)
Bus 63-Dansaert
☎ **512 1176**
Tue.-Sat. 11am-6.30pm.

The key here is layers: shirts, tunics and jackets to wear smartly or casually over a long skirt or baggy trousers. They come in four variations: black, silver grey, white, and Indian prints, from yellow to carmine red and in different fabrics with lots of contrasts – rough and smooth, shiny and matt, transparent and opaque. Great prices which should enable you to buy at least three items all at once. What a bargain!

Putikii

9, Rue de l'Hôpital (HP)
Bus 48-Saint-Jean
☎ **513 9100**
Mon.-Sat. 10am-6pm.

In this shop with a pale wood interior you'll find labels from Scandinavia (Marco Polo, Dranella), Holland (Turnover, Sandwich) and Belgium (Waxx), all of which make clothes for women who aren't shaped like supermodels and hate close-fitting outfits. Well-cut clothes in cotton, wool and linen in which you will feel great. Excellent value for money has brought this shop a loyal clientele.

Nicolas Woit

80, Rue A.-Dansaert (A1)
Metro Bourse
☎ **503 4832**
Tue.-Sat. 12-6pm.

Women who want to escape the constraints of fashion and those who love historical clothes will adore these unconventional creations by this designer trained in Paris. The luxurious fabrics, daring cuts from suits to dresses for special occasions, highly unusual accessories and new items arriving every two weeks will seduce many a shopper. Evening dresses from BF6,500; hats from BF1,500.

Johanne Riss

35, Pl. du Nouveau-Marché-aux-Grains (A1)
Bus 63-Dansaert
☎ **513 0900**
Mon.-Sat 10.30am-6.30pm.

Johanne Riss lives and works in this large white loft with its small inner garden. It's the place to

come to see a line of very feminine garments. You'll find very tight-fitting tapering dresses in Lycra, either very low-cut or with round necks, to wear on their own or with a transparent over-dress and pearls or fabric flowers as

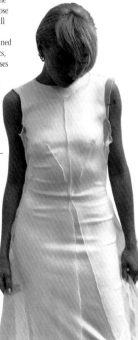

accessories. The wedding dresses are designed in the same spirit with embroidered tulle decorations and silk flowers. Allow BF10,000 for a dress.

Irié

9, Rue Gretry (B1)
Metro De Brouckère
☎ 217 2800
Mon. 1-6.30pm,
Tue.-Sat. 11am-6.30pm.

In this white marble interior you'll find a line of clothes made popular by readers of *Marie-Claire, Elle* and *Cosmopolitan*. They aren't cheap (BF20,000 for an outfit), but you won't regret the investment, particularly as these garments will last several seasons without going out of fashion.

STREET AND CLUBWEAR

Planet One

24A, Av. de la Toison-d'Or (B2)
Metro Porte de Namur
☎ 513 0342
Mon.-Sat. 10.30am-6.30pm.

Flared hipster trousers, tight tops to show off your midriff, stretchy mini-skirts, super-high platform shoes – in other words everything you need in 100% Lycra to dance the night away at a rave, techno club or anywhere else where the music's hot. Mini-prices and maxi-decibel sounds with a DJ every Saturday.

Privejoke

8, Rue des Riches-Claires (A1)
Metro Bourse
☎ 502 7368
Mon.-Sat. 10.30-7pm.

This is the rendezvous for 12-25 year-olds, who drop by clutching their skateboards to pick up their supplies of Carhartt, Lush, Combo, Seda, ÉS etc. Techno and house music in the background, played all day and every day by good DJs, and all the accessories you need, such as Blackflys glasses for snowboarding, stripey belts, fake-crocodile-skin wallets, anti-theft locks and a soft drinks machine too. Cool!

WATCH OUT FOR STAINS!

To return your clothing to its pristine condition after staining, act fast! Blood should be rinsed in plenty of cold water, red wine can be neutralised directly with white wine (salt damages the fibres). Ink can be removed using ordinary soap and water or a mild bleach, and coffee or fruit-juice stains should be rubbed with a cloth dipped in a little vinegar and water or alcohol.

MEN'S FASHIONS

There's nothing like spending a weekend abroad to remind you it's high time you bought yourself some new clothes. Not that the prices here are necessarily better than you'll find at home, but for once you'll actually have the time to try on a new pair of designer trousers and perhaps a Paul Smith shirt, which will give you a totally new look. And on no account should you miss Isabelle Baines's wonderful jumpers.

Balthazar
22, Rue du Marché-aux-Fromages (B1)
Metro Gare Centrale
☎ 514 2396
Mon.-Sat. 11am-6.30pm.

For stylish men's fashions make your way to this charming

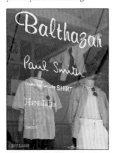

17th-century building a stone's throw from Grand-Place, in a street full of pizza and kebab shops. These garments with Paul Smith, Smedley and Naessens labels are designed for active men who enjoy fashion. The cut, fabric and colour are important with the details making all the difference, from stretch trousers, square collars and coloured buttons to the bright royal blue suit. Items aren't extravagantly priced, but

they also aren't within the range of every budget (polo necks at BF4,000; suits at BF20,000).

Parachute Jump
579, Chaussée de Waterloo (B3)
Bus 60-Tenbosch
☎ 347 4984
Tue.-Sat. 10am-7pm.

This sportswear centre is mainly frequented by women searching for that special gift. The former hardware store with its ostentatious displays is very well-stocked, winter and summer, with shirts of every colour, unusual ties and thousands of accessories for men who want to impress.

Smadja Sport
16, Pl. Brugmann (B3)
☎ 347 6670
Tue.-Sat. 11am-6.30pm,
Sun. 11.30am-3.30pm.

Alongside all the trendy big names you'll also find sportswear designs by Jacques Smadja. These are well cut in a choice of fabrics at truly accessible prices and can be combined with all your indispensable accessories. Friendly sales assistants and a warm atmosphere are the other

strengths of this little centre of men's fashion, which is well worth a visit.

Crossword
504, Gal. de la Toison-d'Or (B2)
Metro Louise or Porte de Namur
☎ 511 0354
Mon.-Sat. 10am-7pm.

A very smart shop where they will kit you out from head to toe in designs by the great names of British and Italian fashion. A dress shirt with double cuffs, every possible design in ties, from plain and classic to the most weird and wonderful, Favour Brook hand-embroidered waistcoats, Tod and Hogan shoes, top-of-the-range, part-tailored suits as well as sportswear items. Expect to pay BF3,500 for a top-quality shirt.

Allen Edmonds

223, Gal. Porte-Louise (B2)
Metro Louise
☎ 511 3563
Mon.-Sat.
10am-
6.30pm.

Nothing but fine American shoes made entirely of leather for every occasion: everyday shoes, mocassins and boots. These shoes are a good alternative to Church's as they're a little less expensive (BF10,000) and they'll last you every bit as long. You'll also find real Docksiders and Sebagos in this shop.

Degand Sport

4, Rue Saint-Georges (B3)
Tram 94-Abbaye
☎ 649 2300
Mon.-Sat. 10am-6.30pm.

A sports department has just been opened at the back of this great made-to-measure specialist. Here you'll find a range of comfortable, tasteful clothes for active men who like to be elegant whatever they're doing. You can have a yellow checked linen jacket or a choice of trousers, cotton jumpers and denim shirts to go with your Tods. The prices are pretty much top-of-the-range too.

Virgin

10, Rue A.-Dansaert (A1)
Metro Bourse
☎ 511 4603
Mon.-Sat. 11am-12.30pm
and 1.30-6.30pm.

This line is at the forefront of the utility/workwear trend: steel-capped heels, under-and-over laces and ring spurs. The label says Dirk Bikkembergs and the range is causing a stir in trendy Flemish circles. The lighter combat boots with square toes and thick soles are also designed to be worn by women.

Church's

2, Pl. Stéphanie (B2)
Tram 94-Stéphanie
☎ 512 4430
Mon.-Sat. 9am-6.30pm.

These are the Rolls Royce of men's shoes. Once your foot has been measured for size, you can buy them without any worries about the fit. The lace-up and buckled styles change very little over time, which

RETURN OF THE DANDY

Are you up with the latest styles? Shoulders should be narrow, waists and armholes close-fitting with big turn-ups on the trousers. Meanwhile fabrics are now brighter and more colourful. No worries these days about using synthetic and natural fibres that are mixed to create elasticity and a moiré effect.

is handy as you can order a new pair from anywhere in the world. They're quite a sizeable investment (BF15,000) but if you look after them properly, you'll keep your pair of Church's for at least 10 years.

CHILDREN'S CLOTHES, SHOES AND TOYS

Whether you're sold on pink frilly layettes and smocked dresses or you prefer a more fashionable look to make your child stand out from the crowd, you'll be spoiled for choice in the many shops for children. Belgian designs don't get exported that much, so your purchases are guaranteed to be quite exclusive back home. When it comes to toy shops, there's really no reason at all why they should be just for children!

Les Casse-Pieds

571, Chaussée de Waterloo (A/B3)
Bus 54-Ma Campagne
☎ 343 2668
Mon.-Sat. 10am-6.30pm and by appt.

Goodbye to boring old brown or white shoes and hello to fashion and colours. These styles are trendy but not vulgar, classy but not classic, in other words a good compromise that pleases both young and old, since what you get is a reduced-size version of the parents' shoes. Here you're guaranteed to find both choice and quality.

Kat en Muis

32, Rue A.-Dansaert (A1)
Metro Bourse
☎ 514 3234
Mon.-Sat. 10.30am-6.30pm.

Here you'll find Dries Van Noten, Paul Smith and Claude Well in miniaturised versions. A very trendy line which has been adapted to suit the little ones, with an age range from 3 months to 16 years. Top-of-the-range means top prices, but given the enormous choice on offer here, you can easily combine styles and prices to suit yourself, for example a basic T-shirt with designer trousers.

Serneels

69, Av. Louise (B2/3)
Tram 94-Stéphanie
☎ 538 3066
Mon.-Sat. 9.30am-6.30pm.

In this very well-stocked shop you'll find costumes to transform your children into Sioux chiefs or fairies. There are rocking horses or racing cars to ride; a theatre with 40 puppets and all kinds of brain-teasing games. All ages from babies to teenagers.

Claude Hontoir

14, Pl. Brugmann (B3)
Bus 60-Brugmann
☎ 346 5947
Tue.-Sat. 11am-6pm and Sun. 11am-4pm.

This designer favours punchy colours and practical, comfortable styles, clothes for everyday wear for babies to pre-teens. The pretty dresses with matching hairbands will turn your daughters' friends green with envy, while for the boys there are Liberto jeans, flannel and jersey trousers, eye-catching jumpers and checked shirts. Expect to pay BF1,500-2,500 for a 6-month-old baby's outfit.

Basile & Boniface

77, Rue de Washington (B3)
Metro Louise
☎ 534 8118
Tue.-Sat. 10.30am-6.30pm.

If you're looking for a hat that's not too old-fashioned for a baby, a little waterproof jacket or fleece, an unusual sweater or some practical outdoor clothing, then this is the place for you. Basile sells clothes for children up to the age of 6 at very reasonable prices in bright citrus colours that bring out their natural healthy glow.

In den Olifant

47, Rue des Fripiers (B1)
Metro De Brouckère
☎ 217 4397
Mon.-Sat. 10am-6.30pm.

Four floors piled high with attractive, original wooden toys. From balsa glider kits to puppets, dolls' houses, farm animals, musical boxes, yachts, Meccano and much, much more. With sizes ranging from tiny to the impossible to carry there's no excuse not to take back a little gift for the kids. Prices from BF89.

Max et Lola

33-34, Gal. Louise (B2)
Metro Louise
☎ 511 8250
Mon.-Sat. 10.30am-6.30pm.

A shop designed with children in mind, full of colour in winter or summer. Glamour and imagination are the inspiration for the collections of clothes for little girls from birth to 14 years and boys up to 10. Fabrics are delicate but practical, apart from the princess dress with its skirt decorated with tulle and ping-pong balls! Prices to match the top-of-the-range styles.

Toy museum

24, Rue de l'Association (B1)
Metro Botanique
☎ 219 6168
Open every day 10am-noon, 2-6pm.

A journey through the world of toys from 1850 to the present day. Attractions include a puppet show in the same room that also houses a very old Belgian tram. Reproductions of old clockwork toys and popular games from around the world (BF100-4,000) are on sale in the shop.

Dujardin

82-84, Av. Louise (B2/3)
Metro Louise
☎ 512 7575
Mon.-Sat. 10am-6.30pm.

In an interior by Gaetano Pece you'll find clothes for well-behaved children aged 0 to 10. There are classic pinafore dresses and bermuda shorts in tartan, stripes and gingham. A good place to find that timeless pink, blue or white layette or a first-communion dress with a big ribbon sash and full sleeves that can be handed down from one child to the next through the generations.

The Plush Corner

8-9, Pl. du Grand-Sablon (B2)
Bus 48-Grand-Sablon
☎ 513 5000
Tue.-Sat. 10am-1pm and 2-6.30pm, Sun. 10am-4pm.

Every possible kind of soft toy from the Steiff label and, for very well-behaved and careful children, collectable teddy bears and vinyl or porcelain dolls in limited editions of 30 to 60. A teddy costs BF3,500-80,000; and a doll BF5,000-130,000!

INTERIOR DECORATION, TABLEWARE AND DESIGN

In your visits to some of the city's trendy restaurants and cafés you'll have noticed that the inhabitants of Brussels are brilliant at interior design. Their homes are larger than the European average and they love high-class furniture, quality materials and beautiful objects, which they display to great effect. If you look carefully, you can find something that's right for you in almost every shop without spending a fortune.

DESIGN

Ligne

12-16, Gal. de la Reine (B1)
Metro Gare Centrale
☎ 511 6030
Mon.-Sat. 10am-6pm.

You'll find all the great names of contemporary design, from F.L. Wright to Jasper Morrison, in this magical shop that draws you irresistibly inside. It's been at the cutting edge of style for 30 years, selling top-of-the-range items only. The exclusive outlet for *Woodnotes* carpets, made in Finland from paper cord at BF6,000/m²/sq. yd. All items are similarly expensive and beautiful.

In Store

90-92, Rue Tenbosch (B3)
Tram 94-Vleurgat
☎ 344 9637
Mon.-Fri. 10am-12.30pm and 2-6.30pm,
Sat. 1-6pm.

A wonderful showroom with daytime, night-time and office spaces filled with contemporary Italian designs (Acerbis, Arflex, Flexform, Boffi). On the second floor you'll find unusual furniture for collectors only, such as Starck's wheelbarrow armchair, at more affordable prices.

FABRICS

Martine Doly

27, Bd de Waterloo (B2)
☎ 512 4628
Metro Louise or Porte de Namur
Mon.-Sat. 10am-6.30pm.

The stables of a former mansion are now the magnificent setting for a range of home furnishing fabrics designed by Martine Doly. Fabrics you'll adore, linen and cotton to spread over your table or bed or to dry your crockery or even yourself with. Also accessories in matching materials and colours such as Alep soaps, Portuguese slippers and jewel cases.

Chintz Shop

35-39, Rue de Rollebeek (B1)
Metro Gare Centrale
☎ 513 5896
Mon.-Fri. 10am-6pm,
Sat. 10.30am-6pm.

The 'shabby chic' style comes direct from LA. You'll be won over by the simplicity and friendly atmosphere of this deliciously old-fashioned shop with its faded flower prints and armchairs with frilly cushions. Crystal chandeliers and a few old ornaments add the finishing touches. Owner Amélie de Borchgrave is on hand to help you with decorative advice.

Kan Dira Ton

158, Rue F.-Merjay (B3)
Bus 60-Brugmann
☎ 346 2844
Mon.-Fri. 10am-6pm,
Sat. 2-6pm.

Ethnic patterns on cotton, velvet, muslin, Swedish prints, coloured weaves from Spain, silk and hand-woven Indian cotton. Quality furnishing fabrics sold by the metre (39 in) in different widths (BF500-2,000 per metre). Rafia blinds and coconut, sisal or jute matting with coloured trim arc among the other specialities of this beautiful shop.

Linen House

10, Rue Bodenbroeck (B2)
Bus 48-Grand-Sablon
☎ 502 6302
Tue.-Sat. 10.30am-12.30pm
and 1.30-6.30pm,
Sun. 10.30am-3pm.

Flemish linen has long had a well-established reputation. This robust yet fine fibre makes wonderful tablecloths and clothes.

This company, which specialises in linen, sells fabric by the metre in large widths as well as dishcloths, tablecloths and napkins in standard sizes. You can also order individualised items including damask, lacy tablecloths or cloths embroidered with your initials. Transportation home of your purchases can also be arranged for you.

HOME DECORATION

Noir d'Ivoire

27, Rue de l'Hôpital (HP)
Bus 48-Saint Jean
☎ 513 5892
Mon.-Sat. 11am-7pm.

If you loved the decor in the *Amadeus* restaurant (see p. 57) then hurry along to Agnès Emery's shop, where you can glean some of her secrets in the three floors decorated in red, yellow and green. Agnès is particularly keen on coloured concrete tiles and Moroccan *zellige*, brocades and velvet and her strong point is colour. Wrought-iron accessories (candlesticks, chairs, consoles),

rafia rugs enlivened with wool and patterned Tamgrout crockery that she has designed or selected complete the picture. Empire fabric at BF1,650 per metre/yard; fruit bowl at BF650.

Isabelle de Borchgrave

27, Rue de Rollebeek (B2)
Bus 48-Grand-Sablon
☎ 514 3639
Tue.-Sat. 10.30am-6.30pm,
Sun. 11am-2.30pm.

Isabelle de Borchgrave is an interior designer and true artist. The freshness of her bouquets and still lifes, combined with elements of calligraphy, can be found in all kinds of places: on her textiles of course (from voile to carpets), but also on furniture, crockery, walls, wallpapers and mirror frames. One visit to her home-cum-shop and you can redesign your entire interior, or just buy a tablecloth, hand-painted curtain or one of her pictures at prices which are far from extravagant.

New De Wolf

91, Rue Haute (A/B2)
Bus 20 and 48-Chapelle
☎ 511 1018
Mon.-Sat. 10am-6.30pm,
Sun. 10am-3pm.

An enormous home hypermarket laid out according to such themes as Africa, Tuscany, Asia, the English look, on the beach and in the garden. The stock is constantly updated, which means there's new things to explore and you can redesign your home at bargain prices. Proof that beautiful things don't have to be expensive.

Baltazar

100, Rue de Stassart (B2)
Metro Porte de Namur
☎ 512 8513
Tue.-Sat. 10am-7pm,
Sun. 11am-5pm.

If you'd like to treat yourself to an Alechinsky lithograph, an engraving by Gabriel Belgeonne, Pompon's white bear or a Khmer Buddha's head, well you can! This is the art bazaar where you'll find a mix of resin reproductions of works of art from the great museums and original works by Belgian and foreign artists. For BF500-50,000, you can buy works that will enhance your home and turn your guests green with envy.

Esprit de Famille

478, Rue Vanderkindere (HP)
Tram 92-Vanderkindere
☎ 345 3179
Tue.-Sat. 10.30am-1pm and 2.30-6.30pm.

If you're looking to replace the shade on your 1950s lamp, or you'd like a lamp stand made from a little bronze statue or a Chinese vase, you've come to the right place. You're bound to find the very

thing among the enormous range of lamps available here.

Argus Corp.

11-13 Rue Van Moer (B2)
Tram 93/94
☎ 511 2835
Tue.-Sat. 11am-noon and 2-5pm, Sun. 11am-1pm.

Superb cut crystal glasses dated 1900-1950 from Val Saint

Lambert. Here you can replace the ones you've broken or buy a complete set at half price. If your dinner guests are on the clumsy side this shop is the answer to your prayers. You'll also find pieces by Gallé, Daum and Lalique.

Flamant

32, Pl. du Grand-Sablon (B2)
Bus 48-Grand-Sablon
☎ 514 4707
Mon.-Sat. 10.30am-6.30pm,
Sun. 10.30am-3pm.

There's everything here, from sofas to glasses, candlesticks, china and Chinese stoneware, wooden ducks and seagulls, bowls, models of the Honfleur lighthouse, French-polished furniture, English pottery and Royal Boch crockery. There are armchairs made of fine rattan, tables, baskets and boxes and cast-iron silhouettes to use as doorstops. All kinds of lovely objects from BF500.

FOR YOUR TABLE

Terrachiara

1 069, Chaussée de Waterloo (A/B3)
Bus 368-Vert Chasseur
☎ 374 6813
Mon.-Sat. 10.30am-7pm,
Tue. and Sun. by appt.

Step inside and you're instantly transported to Tuscany. There are fruit and flowers everywhere decorating white enamel flowerpot

Dille & Kamille
16, Rue Jean-Stas (B2)
Metro Louise
☎ 538 8125
Mon.-Sat. 9.30am-6.30pm.

As soon as the sun comes out, the pavement is covered in pots full of artichokes, sunflowers and aromatic herbs, giving you a hint of the fragrances to be enjoyed in this wonderful shop which specialises in cooking utensils. Iron, wooden or stainless steel spoons, lemon squeezers, ice-cream servers, strawberry hullers, dozens of cake-tins in different shapes, enamel crockery perfect for picnics all at prices to confound the competition.

holders, columns, trays, fruit bowls, chandeliers and vases; there are bunches of gleaming fruits to hang on the wall and magnificent *cesti frutta* or ceramic fruit baskets to decorate your table. For the garden you'll find big pots decorated with garlands to set you dreaming of planting a lemon tree.

take the opportunity to smash a few plates, just for fun. All the same, the English china dinner services (30 pieces at BF1,495) are absolutely beautiful, just like the cast-iron chandeliers, candleholders and cotton tablecloths. Thousands of ideas to brighten up your table, such as glass fish (BF60) and silver-plated toast-racks at BF595.

Côté Vaisselle
46, Rue de Stassart (B2)
Metro Porte de Namur
☎ 513 7608
Mon.-Sat. 10am-6.30pm.

At the kind of prices they're charging for the crockery on display in this renovated warehouse you could almost

A ROYAL BOCH DINNER SERVICE

The Royal Boch factory, founded in 1841 in La Louvière, is still making crockery which is highly prized for the quality of its china, a mix of clay and kaolin, with all the solidity of porcelain. The pieces are decorated using transfers, which are sometimes retouched by hand and are permanently fixed by the second firing at 1,140°C. Prices are double for *Copenhagen* crockery (a design of fine blue lines) and *Rangoon* (plain with beading). Period pieces are much sought-after.

DELICIOUS TREATS

In Brussels it's traditional to take a *ballotin* of pralines (a box of chocolates) as a gift when you're invited to someone's house. To save you from the embarassment of giving a brand you can now buy in a supermarket, here are some places you can be sure of finding the best products in the city at prices distinctly lower than those you'll pay elsewhere. Don't forget that chocolates generally travel pretty well too.

Mary
73, Rue Royale (B1)
Bus 63-Congrès
☎ 217 4500
Tue.-Fri. 9am-6pm,
Sat. 9am-5pm.

This chocolate supplier to the royal family, situated opposite the Congress column, is now in the hands of the third generation, with the wife selling the produce made by her husband. Everything is done by hand, including whipping the cream. Blue and gold decor and very dark chocolate is used, ranging from very sweet to bitter with 99.7% cocoa. While a less fatty milk chocolate than usual is tolerated, white chocolate is banned. There are handy cool bags to hold the chocolates, which are four times the price of their mass-produced rivals, but incomparably better.

Neuhaus
25-27, Gal. de la Reine (B1)
Metro Gare Centrale
☎ 512 6359
Mon.-Sat. 10am-8pm,
Sun. 10am-5pm.

The inventor of the concept of the *ballotin* and of the name 'praline' is one of the oldest Belgian chocolate manufacturers. His top products are *caprice* and *tentation* ('temptation'), which are nougatines filled with fresh cream. Success has led to the opening of several further outlets in key locations throughout the city. The price per kilo of his delicious pralines is a lot less than elsewhere (BF1,080).

Irsi
15, Rue du Bailli (B3)
Bus 54-Trinité
☎ 648 7050
Mon.-Sat. 8.30am-7pm.

An old-fashioned confectioner's with rows of jars full of *manons* – sweets covered in white chocolate and filled with fresh cream.

Manons come in various flavours: vanilla, mocha, Grand Marnier, cognac and Napoleon Mandarin. Other specialities include less-rich fruit creams and orangettes (chocolate with orange peel). A kilo of chocolates will cost you BF1,000, a kilo of fruit creams BF700.

Corné Toison d'Or

24-26, Gal. du Roi (B1)
Metro Gare Centrale
☎ 512 4984
Mon.-Sat. 9.30am-7pm
and Sun. 10.30am-6.30pm.

For a real treat ask for an assortment of *mendiants* – chocolate with dried fruit and almonds – and *florentines*, biscuits with almonds, honey and very dark chocolate. Then throw in a few sugar-coated pralines or marzipan *Manons*. These delicious chocolates cost BF980 a kg.

Godiva

89, Bd A.-Max (B1)
Metro Rogier
☎ 217 3514
Tue.-Sat. 10am-6pm.

This internationally renowned confectioner specialises in pralines made from Turkish hazelnuts, which are ground and mixed with slivers of nougatine, grilled almonds and hazelnuts. Godiva has developed a range of 16 varieties whose flavour gradually develops in your mouth. Other musts are the *caraques*, little squares of very dark chocolate, and truffles, chocolate and butter creams dusted with cocoa. A kilo of pralines costs BF1,190.

Dandoy

31, Rue au Beurre (A1)
Metro Bourse
☎ 511 0326
Mon.-Sat. 8.30am-6.30pm,
Sun. and hols 10.30am-6.30pm.

Belgium's oldest biscuit-makers, where all the products are made by hand. Hard to choose between the *speculoos*, *massepain*, *pain à la grecque* and *pain d'épices*. On the other hand the *couques de Dinant* are used as kitchen decorations and are eaten only in time of famine.

De Boe

36, Rue de Flandre (A1)
Metro Sainte-Catherine
☎ 511 1373
Tue.-Fri. 9am-1pm and
2-6pm, Sat. 9am-6pm.

The taste has been passed down from generation to generation, from great-grandfather Cyrille, who first opened his grinding business in 1896. The machine is still in action every morning, giving off the lovely aroma of pure arabica coffee. You'll also find blended teas, green tea with cardamon, cornflower tea, and many other delicious things, including Valrhona chocolate, *tartuffo* and capers with sea salt.

Le Déjeuner sur l'Herbe

6, Av. Lepoutre (B3)
Bus 60-Tenbosch
☎ 346 1759
Tue.-Sun. 11am-8pm.

An old-fashioned local grocer's in a chemist's shop, where you'll find gift ideas for your foodie friends. *Waterzoï* and homemade preserves of rabbit with *faro* are delicious, and don't miss out on the sauces and pesto made by an Italian living in Belgium, or the delicious organic bread. The staff are charming.

A ROMAN TRADITION

Pliny the Elder noted that good children were rewarded with gifts of cakes made of flour and honey in the shape of gods from the Roman Pantheon. It was almost certainly Roman legionnaires who introduced these treats into Gaul, where they still bring joy to children. On the eve of 6 December, St Nicholas' day, slippers are hung by every chimney, waiting to be filled with sweets in exchange for a few carrots for the saint's donkey. Of course they're only given to good children…

GIFTS AND PRESENTS

Little models of Tintin or Mannekenpis aren't the only souvenirs you can take home with you from this city that has a true passion for objects. From the weird to the wonderful, exotic or fun, here are some addresses where you can find an original present for a friend or something that will always remind you of your visit to Brussels.

Dans la Presse ce Jour-là

23, Rue du Lombard (A1)
Metro Bourse
☎ 511 4389
Mon.-Fri. 11.30am-6.30pm, Sat. 11.30am-5pm.

If you'd like to know what was happening in the world on the day you were born, why not buy a Belgian newspaper, as long as you were born after 1895! For friends a bottle of port or Armagnac

produced the year they were born will always make a welcome gift. Of course it's better for your wallet if none of the recipients are a hundred years old. Or what about a family chronicle, a gigantic hand-bound book full of documents and photographs displaying life's important moments. A splendid gift for a golden wedding or similar occasion.

Z'Art

223A, Chaussée d'Ixelles (B2/C3)
Bus 71-F. Cocq
☎ 649 0653
Tue.-Sat. 11am-7pm.

Magritte and Picabia would have loved these objects, whose shape bears no relation to their function. The cow is a rubber plug, the broom handle zigzags, there's a hard latex tie and a foam rubber telephone. Everything is odd and amusing. Full of fun gift ideas from BF50-10,000.

La Boutique de Tintin

13, Rue de la Colline (B1)
Metro Gare Centrale
☎ 514 5152
Mon.-Sat. 10am-6pm, Sun. and hols 11am-7pm.

Even if you're not a fan of the little reporter and his faithful dog, Snowy, you'll find some unusual items here. A very smart 'Rakkham the red' breakfast service, a reproduction of the idol of the Arumbayas and *Tintin* in Japanese. But it's all rather expensive.

Brussels Corner

27, Rue de l'Étuve (A1)
Metro Bourse
☎ 511 9849
Open every day 9am-10.30pm in summer, until 7pm in winter.

Do you fancy buying a Mannekenpis to uncork your bottles? If you must buy the traditional souvenir, then you might as well make use of it – and have you actually seen the statue of this little boy peeing on a street corner?

Matière Première

52, Rue du Bailli (B3)
Bus 54-Trinité
☎ 649 7290
Tue.-Sat. 11am-6.30pm.

A little shop with a *trompe l'œil* decor where the colours and materials change with the seasons. So you'll find raffia table mats, Moroccan tea glasses and beach towels in summer, and gold candles, glass balls and Icelandic wool in winter. There are pretty notebooks made from Nepalese paper, dishes in black Colombian pottery and loads of other items to fill your home all year round.

Boulot

188, Rue Josaphat (HP)
Bus 65/66-Coteaux
☎ 241 0127.

All the characters of Brussels' folklore that you've seen in pictures at *Toone*'s, represented in the Ommegang, in the flesh in Marolles or in cartoons, are immortalised here as puppets. *Quick and Flupke, Agent 15*, the *Prole from Marolles*, *Wooden Legged Charlie* and *Emperor Charles V* are all on sale for BF795-995.

Bougie Gommers

994, Chaussée de Waterloo (B3)
Bus 366-Vert Chasseur
☎ 375 3438
Tue.-Fri. 10am-6pm,
Sat. 10am-3pm.

Happily the arrival of electricity hasn't affected the business of this family, who've been working wax since 1893. In this little shop you'll find a candle for every occasion, from church candles to candles in the shape of easter eggs, star-signs, cauliflowers, champagne bottles, Buddhas as well as souvenir candles like a beer mug, a Brussels' paving stone and, of course, Mannekenpis!

Eurotempo

84, Rue du Marché-aux-Herbes (B1)
Metro Gare Centrale
☎ 230 6271
Open every day 10am-7pm.

It's no longer just the Eurocrats who shelter under a star-spangled royal blue umbrella. Now you can get the 18-star European logo on socks, T-shirts, watches, bags and Swiss army-style knives. And if you want to get to know the new currency in a hurry, why not treat yourself to some chocolate Euros?

ALSO TRY:

100% Design
30, Bd Anspach (A/B1)
☎ 219 6198, Tue.-Sat. 10am-6.30pm and Mon. noon-6.30pm. The home of inflatables.

Rosalie Pompon
65, Rue Lebeau (B2)
☎ 512 3593, Tue.-Sun. 10.30am-6pm.
Hilarious gift ideas.

Graphie Sud
15, Pl. Brugmann (B3)
☎ 344 3192, Tue.-Sat. 11am-6.30pm, Sun. 11.30am-3.30pm.
Jewellery, clothes and objects from around the world.

ANTIQUES

Anyone will tell you that Brussels is one of the hubs of the antiques market. The sales rooms are packed with foreign buyers who come to find real bargains, so make sure you do the rounds of the antiques shops and don't hesitate to ask the price of an item if it isn't displayed. You'll be amazed to find that pieces of furniture and other objects may cost as little as half what you'd pay back home. The dealers' secret lies in the city's low rents and a very high turnover, which means they're always renewing their stock. Remember, too, that not all the best shops are in Sablon and that it's seldom a problem to have furniture sent abroad.

Au Fil du Temps

41, Rue Lebeau (B2)
Bus 20-Grand-Sablon
☎ 513 3487
**Mon.-Sat. 11am-1pm
and 2-6pm.**

A good place to find high-quality 19th-century bronzes: Carpeaux and, if you're lucky, maybe even a Rodin. Berkowitsch also specialises in period Royal Boch ceramics and Austrian furniture from the early years of the 20th century.

Atmosphères

17, Rue de Rollebeek (B2)
Bus 20-Grand-Sablon
☎ 513 1110
**Tue.-Sat. 11am-6pm,
Sun. 11am-2pm.**

If you feel nostalgic for the colonies and love 19th-century French and English furniture, make sure you visit this dealer, who buys only what he likes himself. Indian lanterns hanging from the ceiling, portraits and hunting trophies on the walls and,

dotted around on the furniture, numerous ornaments and unusual objects that would look perfect in your home. Prices from BF1,500-150,000.

Carpe Diem and l'Authentique

19, Rue des Minimes (B2)
Bus 48-Grand-Sablon
☎ 503 4850
**Tue.-Sat. 11am-1pm and
2-6pm, Sun. 11am-2pm.**

Dive into the world of rural life with its old-fashioned values. As well as some lovely Berry stoneware you'll find furniture, lighting and mirrors unearthed from the depths of the French countryside (early 19th- to 20th-century). And the prices aren't over the top either.

Faisons un Rêve

112, Av. Lepoutre (B3)
Bus 60-Brugmann
☎ 347 3429
**Tue.-Sat. 10.30am-6.30pm,
Wed. 2-6.30pm.**

This is the perfect shop if you love Art Deco. Here, depending on your budget, you can find a 1920s picture frame, a manicure set with all the accessories in white bakelite, a chrome-plated lamp stand or an entire drawing-room, but you won't go away empty-handed. Everything has been beautifully restored, and you can have the armchairs restuffed. The prices are very affordable, but you'll need to think about transportation.

Orient Antiques

88, Rue de Namur (B2)
Metro Porte de Namur
☎ 511 2711
Mon.-Sat. 10.30am-6pm.

This dealer is rightly renowned for his great professionalism. The furniture is Japanese or Chinese, the statues and objects are from southeast Asia. Everything is

magnificent and expensive (large Chinese wardrobes from BF95,000-125,000) but authenticity is guaranteed. You can also treat the gallery like a museum, as there is an explanatory card identifying every item. If you can't afford to buy, you can still educate yourself while admiring the beautiful objects.

Nicholson

131, Rue Franz-Merjay (B3)
Bus 60-Brugmann
☎ 343 8682
Mon.-Sat. 2.30-7pm.

Mahogany and leather, a very masculine and terribly British emporium, which is just what you'd expect from this dealer who specialises in Victorian furniture. Models of transatlantic liners and Americas Cup yachts, golf bags and other luxurious items from far and wide, all of impeccable taste and quality.

Horta salesroom

70-74 Av. de Roodebeek (D1)
Metro Diamant
☎ 741 6060
Viewing Fri. 2-8pm,
Sat. 10am-7pm,
Sun. 10am-6.30pm.
Sales Mon. and Tue. 7.30pm
except July and Aug.

Both for connoisseurs in the know and for the occasional visitor, an auction is always exciting and unique. Find out the viewing dates for the monthly sale before you plan your weekend. If you can't make the sale itself, you can send in a written order or arrange a telephone line. You need to add 20% in charges to the auction price, and possibly

3 to 6% additional copyright fees for a sculpture or painting. If you have access to the internet, you can always zoom in on a digital image of the object of your dreams.

CHINESE AND JAPANESE FURNITURE: THE RIGHT PRICE

You'll no doubt be amazed to find the Chinese wardrobe you saw in a reputable dealer's shop sold at a quarter or fifth of the price by another trader. You need to remember that the price of Asian furniture largely relys on the wood it's made from, with sandalwood the most valuable and pine the least. Next in importance comes the age of the piece and last but not least, the quality of the restoration. A piece of furniture that's been left in damp conditions may well split in a dry, heated environment if it hasn't been treated properly. If you're interested in quality Japanese antique furniture, go straight to a restorer and cabinet-maker:
Stefan Geyns
858, Chaussée d'Alsemberg (A3).
☎ 376 8912.
Tram 55-Rittweger.
By appointment only.

SECONDHAND GOODS

If you've been foolish enough to throw away all your old clothes from the 1970s, don't panic! There are loads of places specialising in flares, platform shoes and checked trousers. However, if it's a classic item you're after, such as a fur coat or a Chanel suit, you'll find these are also available in the more upmarket secondhand shops.

L'Homme Chrétien
27, Rue des Pierres (A1)
Metro Bourse
☎ 502 0128
Mon.-Sat. 11am-7pm.

The art of turning old into new – or how to transform an old quilted dressing-gown into an elegant jacket! Alongside his more unusual creations and a few remnants from his mystic period, Bernard Gavilan sells old stocks of unworn clothes (corduroy and flared trousers, tracksuits)

and a very good selection of secondhand clothes, from miniskirts to leather jackets from the seventies.

R & V
19, Rue des Teinturiers (A1)
Bus 48-Plattesteen
☎ 511 0510
Mon.-Sat. 11am-7pm.

In Ramon and Valy's shop you'll find unique designer items (Chanel, Lanvin, YSL, Dries Van Noten) secondhand at around

BF2,000, as well as new or used clothes from the 1950s to 1970s for adults and children of both sexes. Sallick jeans at BF1,000, checked jackets and coats with fun-fur collars.

Look 50
10, Rue de la Paix (B2)
Metro Porte de Namur
☎ 512 2418
Mon.-Sat. 10am-6.30pm.

All the fashions from the 1950s to the 1970s for both sexes with an emphasis on American cocktail dresses (BF750-2,000), leather coats (BF3,500), hats (BF500-700) and genuine secondhand Levi 501s imported from the United States (BF1,990). You can also get a complete dinner suit for BF3,800,

dresses with crinolines, bags and Hollywood-style sunglasses for those smart evening events. Should you also need something for the more casual events you'll find good old hand-knitted jumpers and hippy dresses.

Idiz Bogam II
76, Rue A.-Dansaert (A1)
Metro Bourse
☎ 512 1032
Mon.-Sat. 10.30am-6.30pm.

It's a fairly simple step from dealing in luxury secondhand goods to design, and Jacqueline has made that step. In her shop, near the outlets of the major designers of the Antwerp school,

SECONDHAND GOODS ■ 101

you'll find a large secondhand section selling clothes for men as well as ballgowns from the 1940s to the 1970s with all the accessories (BF2,800-7,000), and copies of clothes and shoes from the 1970s.

AMANDINE

150, Rue Defacqz (B2/3)
Tram 92-Janson
☎ **539 1793**
Mon.-Sat. 10am-6pm.

If you want to be the belle of the ball, either at your

wedding, or just at an evening out dancing, but you've only got a limited budget, you can hire your outfit here. There are wedding dresses fit for a princess, with crinolines, trains, tulle sewn with pearls and lace for BF7,000; taffeta dresses draped with organdie for BF2,900 and superb costume jewellery and evening bags.

Ribambelle

39, Rue du Bailli (B3)
Bus 54-Trinité
☎ **649 8244**
Mon. 1-6pm,Tue.-Sat. 10.30am-6pm.

This is more than just a shop selling secondhand children's clothes. There are new books at half price and secondhand cartoon

books, novels, board games, toys and school equipment at very good prices. The savings mean you can buy your little one a treat like a fantastic Tex Avery watch. A shop where you don't have to watch your wallet.

Les Enfants d'Édouard

175-177 A, Av. Louise (B3)
Tram 94-Defacqz
☎ **640 4245**
Mon.-Sat. 9.30am-6.30pm.

This, the crème de la crème of secondhand shops, fills two grand mansions, one for women, the other for the men. Inside you'll encounter only high-class punters who've dropped in for an Armani suit, a Boss coat, Chanel suit or Gaultier dress. Even the accessories have labels (jewellery by Christian Lacroix, Hermès ties). None of the clothes are more than two years old and are, it goes without saying, in excellent condition.

Michèle Simon

128, Gal. Louise (B2)
Tram 94-Stéphanie
☎ **512 3389**
Mon.-Sat. 10am-6.30pm.

A warehouse for smart, classic women who like to renew their wardrobes

regularly. Mink coats at BF40,000, Natan and YSL suits (BF6,500), Olivier Strelli dresses and Hermès scarves. All the clothes have designer labels and are good as new, including the maternity garments. It may take a few visits to find something really special.

Boutique de Caroline

27, Rue de l'Amazone (B3)
Bus 54-Trinité
☎ **537 3003**
Mon.-Sat. 10am-6pm.

Designer clothes in top condition for children and mothers-to-be, items from the Babeurre and Farfelu collections and ends of lines from Hilde & Co. sporting the Geluck cat in lots of fun versions.

DISCOUNT STORES: THE ART OF BARGAIN-HUNTING

You don't have to wait for the sales to come round to treat yourself to designer goods. In these stores you can buy two or three garments for the price of one, and they won't be more than a season old. Set aside at least one suitcase to take your weekend's purchases home with you, and if you're buying discount furniture, remember it may be the transportation home that costs the most.

Pour Vous Messieurs

33, Rue Tenbosch (B3)
Tram 93/94-Lesbroussart
☎ 646 3679
Tue.-Sat. 10.30am-6.30pm.

With all-leather shoes from the great Italian and English brands (Mario Bruni, Sebago, Loak, Henry Scott) available at discount prices all year round, your trip to Brussels could turn out to have paid for itself. A wide range of styles and sizes is available from BF3,000.

Michel de Mulder & The Stock

11, Rue Léon Lepage (A1)
Bus 63-Dansaert
☎ 512 5533
Mon. 1.30-6.30pm,
Wed.-Sat. 11am-6.30pm.

At the back of the shop they sell ends of lines from avant-garde designers (Soho, Mieke Cosyn, Kaat Tilley, Eva Lacres) at half the usual price all year round. In the main area you may fall for the truly special made-to-measure shirts and suits created by Michel de Mulder. There's also

a wide range of wedding dresses by Mieke Cosyn.

Dod Femme

44, Chaussée de Louvain (C1)
Metro Madou
☎ 218 2468
Mon.-Sat. 10am-6.30pm.

The most low-key shop of all time. There is no effort at interior design and morose sales assistants, yet it does a roaring trade. Of course all the brands (including big names like Chantal Thomass and Cardin) are sold at a minimum 50% discount. The stock is all last season's or last year's collections, in good condition, all lumped together for the browser's pleasure, particularly in the sales periods when it's all even cheaper. What more could you ask for?

Dod Homme

16, Chaussée de Louvain (C1)
Metro Madou
☎ 218 0454
Mon.-Sat. 10am-6.30pm.

Following their enormous success with their women's shop, Dod have taken on the men's market. Calvin Klein briefs and trousers, Ralph Lauren at bargain prices, designer shoes, singlets and swimming

trunks, superb Laurentis and Hechter jackets and leather jackets (for BF5,000!). Not forgetting discounted Samsonite luggage for carrying home all your purchases.

Dod Junior

41, Chaussée de Louvain (C1)
Metro Madou
☎ 217 5208
Mon.-Sat. 10am-6.30pm.

Here you can dress your little ones from head to toe without worrying about your wallet. In fact, you begin to wonder why on earth you should go to Jacadi, Donaldson or Ale Oli to pay twice the price. The packaging here isn't so fancy and the choice is more haphazard, but you'll have all the fun of the hunt while the kids will have a whale of a time playing hide and seek in this unconventional store.

G. N. A. P.

12-14, Rue du Beffroi (C2)
☎ 732 8473
Mon.-Sat. 10am-6pm.

So you love Max Mara but you haven't got the patience to wait for the sales? Items from the collection (garments from the catwalks and press shows) are sold 40% cheaper all year round. The shop is spotless and busy, the stock is continually renewed and you'll also find (even cheaper) unsold or bankruptcy stock, sub-brands of Max Mara and designs by Marina Rinaldi.

Superdesign

410, Chaussée de Waterloo (A/B3)
Bus 54-Ma Campagne
☎ 534 0367
Mon.-Fri. 11am-6pm, Sat. 10am-5pm, closed Wed.

Ends of lines from Italian designers at very good prices, as long as you're not trying to furnish an entire room. The stock consists mainly of lamps, chairs and occasional tables, which you should purchase immediately if you don't want to miss out on a bargain.

Degrif

49, Rue Simonis (B3)
Bus 54-Trinité
☎ 537 5304
Mon.-Sat. 10.30am-7pm.

Here you'll find the major brands of Italian and French shoes at half price. Everything on sale is always new, either from bankruptcy sales or ends of lines, and comes in every size. There are handmade styles for men, lovely leather shoes for women and sports styles for children.

In other words, there's something here for every member of the family. No wonder the shop is always crowded.

Dépôt Design

16, Rue de la Buanderie (A3)
Metro Anneessens
☎ 502 2882
Tue.-Sat. 10.30am-6.30pm.

This is an old printworks where contemporary furniture, designed by major Italian and Belgian designers, is sold at a discount. Furniture and items from exhibitions, ends of lines and imports direct from the factory, all new or nearly new. The place to buy a small lamp, bookshelf or sofa.

Store Limited

8-10 Rue Bucholtz (B3)
Tram 93/94-Vleurgat
☎ 644 2266
Tue.-Sat. 11am-7pm, Sun. noon-7pm.

This large warehouse in the smart Ixelles district is always extremely busy. Here sharp young men from Gotha sell the latest collections of sportswear and garments in classic styles for men, women and children from the big names at a discount (30 to 40% cheaper). The chances of finding a bargain in the home department aren't quite as good, but since you've come all this way you might as well take a look. You never know, you might find something you like there.

BOOKSHOPS

Ever since the day Brussels was founded, there has always been a fascination and need for images that transcend the language barriers. For this reason, pride of place in the bookshops goes to illustration: art books, comics, photographic magazines, lithographs, postcards and reproductions of every kind, even images printed on objects.

Posada

29, Rue de la Madeleine (B1)
Metro Gare Centrale
☎ 511 0834
Tue.-Sat. 10am-12.30pm and 1.30-6pm.

Here you'll find everything, or nearly everything, related to the history of art. The three floors of this narrow building are filled from floor to ceiling with rare and luxury editions, secondhand and out-of-print books and recent and old catalogues. The sales staff have encyclopaedic knowledge and, if the work you want isn't on the shelves, they'll scour the world for it for you.

Histoires

76, Coudenberg (B1)
Metro Parc
☎ 513 9990
Mon.-Sat. 10am-6.30pm, Sun. 11am-6pm.

A friendly bookshop that's open on Sundays, where you can browse your way to a greater knowledge of Brussels, Belgium or history in general. The staff's own selections of the best new novels

and art history books are laid out on the tables. Foreign newspapers and magazines are also on sale.

Artemys

8, Gal. Bortier (B1)
Metro Gare Centrale
☎ 512 0347
Tue.-Thu. 10am-6pm, Fri. and Sat. 10am-7pm, 15 July-15 Sep. from noon.

This feminist bookstore has a huge range of books on art, the social sciences and fiction, as well as a wide selection of lesbian literature in French, Flemish and English. It also sells calendars and has one of the most extensive postcard collections in the whole of Brussels.

La Bande des Six Nez

179, Chaussée de Wavre (B2/C2)
Bus 96-Parnasse
☎ 513 7258
Mon.-Sat. 10.30am-7pm.

Everyone gets a 20% discount here. Besides a pretty wide range of comics from around the world, there's a secondhand section and a few collector's items which are shown only to people who express an interest. It's a shame that the shop's expansion seems to have been used entirely to sell models and other comic-strip merchandise.

Brüsel

100, Bd Anspach (A1)
Metro Bourse
☎ 502 3552
Mon.-Sat. 10.30am-6.30pm,
Sun. noon-6.30pm.

'Brüsel' means 'Schuiten', which means quality comics. The mezzanine houses a permanent exhibition of signed and numbered screen prints while on the ground floor there are 5,500 new and advance issue titles and some merchandise (watches, bags, lighters) with images of Corto Maltese and Bilal's heroes. If you buy a comic you automatically receive a quarterly magazine that keeps you up-to-date on all the comic news.

Univers Particulier

194, Chaussée de Charleroi (B2)
Tram 92-Faider
☎ 538 1777
Mon.-Sat. 10am-7pm.

If you're interested in knowledge of the occult, dowsing, radionics and magnetism or you believe in tarot cards, astrology and numerology and you'd like to know what happens when we die, then pay Univers Particulier a visit. Set your thinking to positive, buy some incense with special powers and dive into this strange world at the frontiers of reality.

Sans Titre

8, Av. de Stalingrad (A3)
Metro Annessens
☎ 514 2512
Mon.-Sat. 11am-6.30pm.

Here you'll find absolutely all the comics that are on the market and a good selection of books for young people. They care about books here, so the selection favours quality cartoons and small publishers. Regular exhibitions by cartoonists and illustrators.

Ziggourat

34, Rue Dejoncker (B2)
Metro Louise
☎ 538 4037
Tue.-Sat. 11am-6.30pm.

As well as a beautiful shop where they sell comics, this is a venue where there's always something going on, including monthly exhibitions of original plates by cartoonists or illustrators, exhibitions on themes such as *Alice in Wonderland*, and 'signing brunches'. Collectors should look out for the screen prints on Plexiglas and highly individualised letters in the guise of ex-libris stickers. There's even a bronze sculpture by Frank, all in limited editions of course.

BRAS TO BOXERS

Use your weekend as an excuse to take the man in your life to a lingerie store. He can't fail to respond to the delicate, sophisticated, sensual or even wicked wares on offer, whether made from silk or satin, and you're bound to come out with a gift. In return you can always buy him those silk pyjamas he's been secretly dreaming of, or designer underwear to make him even more desirable.

Rosebud

48, Rue Rollebeek (B1)
Metro Gare Centrale
☎ 514 0851
Tue.-Sat. 11am-7pm, Sun. 11am-3pm.

Polished parquet floor and heavy damask hangings, a beautiful setting to show off some extremely delicate lingerie for day or night wear including lovely lace negligées and embroidered ensembles. A wide range of swimwear, both one-piece and bikinis, will make you stand out from the crowd on the beach. Tifa will help you lace up your bustier, but once you've bought it you'll have to ask your partner to do it! Expensive (BF2,500-7,000 for a bra) but delicious.

Stijl Underwear

47, Rue A.-Dansaert (A1)
Metro Bourse
☎ 514 2731
Mon.-Sat. 10.30am-6.30pm.

The place to buy original, unusual and fun lingerie for women and men in a shop whose interior screams 'design'. A selection of the most exclusive styles from each brand, including a bra made of real wire by André Sarda and the pair of orange men's briefs with little pockets for your lighter or condoms. Nightshirts you could just as well wear during the day, silk pyjamas and well-cut swimwear, and you even get to try them on in cubicles worthy of a film star.

Coup de Folie

19, Pl. Brugmann (B3)
Bus 60-Brugmann
☎ 344 0007
Mon.-Sat. 10.30am-6.30pm.

A very pleasant shop which dresses girls, their mothers and mature ladies. There's something to suit every purse, and every size from tiny to the very large, with hundreds of styles in each size. Their range is phenomenal, not to mention the swimwear (stunning one-pieces and bikinis) and nightwear (baby-doll nighties, silk and cotton negligées and much more). The atmosphere is relaxed and they'd rather you tried on 50 bras than just one. An excellent shop where every woman will find something to suit her.

Pierrel

6-10, Gal. du Centre (A1)
Metro Bourse
☎ 223 1050
Mon.-Sat. 10.30am-6pm.

To keep up with all the latest trends, from close-fitting boxers to briefs with horizontal openings, or to treat yourself to a great bathrobe, look no further. This is the only shop in Brussels to stock such a wide range of underwear, pyjamas and swimwear for men. Always in the forefront of fashion and always in good taste, it sells around twenty big names, including Calvin Klein, Armani, Hom and Olaf Beuz.

Minuit Boutique

60, Gal. du Centre (A1)
Metro Bourse
☎ 223 0914
Mon.-Sat. 10.30am-6.30pm.

At last, truly torrid underwear for women! Vinyl, leather and imitation leather, even some in

lace, but all in the most original and outlandish styles. Are you really ready for the baby-doll nightie in black and fluorescent red plastic, the spider bra or the tulle coat that is worn over a leather corset with mega-high platform shoes? Connoisseurs will be able to find all their favourite S&M accessories, and other outrageous underwear.

Champagne et Caviar

40, Gal. du Centre (A1)
Metro Bourse
☎ 219 7582
Mon.-Sat. 11am-6.30pm.

If you're out to seduce a prince, hurry along to this little shop, as it's here that Prince Fily buys underwear. Two designers, one male, one female, have let their fantasies run riot with the aim of fulfilling yours. The result is a range of lingerie with a very hard look, leather, vinyl and imitation leopardskin or snakeskin, as well as tight-fitting miniskirts and body-hugging tops.

Prices aren't excessive: you could easily kit yourself out with an ensemble from as little as BF2,000.

PATRICIA SHOP

158, Rue Blaes (A2)
Bus 48-Jeu de Balle
☎ 513 3648
Tue.-Sat. 9.30am-6pm,
Sun. 9.30am-1pm.

There's nothing very flashy about the window display and yet, if you look carefully among all the lace and leopardskin prints, you're bound to find a Sloggi body stocking, an Erès swimming costume or a La Perla brassiere that will look fantastic on you. Styles from bankruptcy sales and ends of lines may be a season out of date, but when you think that you can buy three for the price of one, why deprive yourself?

ACCESSORIES

Even if you buy your clothes from a high street store, there's nothing to stop you wearing an eye-catching designer scarf or piece of jewellery. The trick is in the detail. So why not invest in a beautiful pair of leather gloves, a designer diary or a fashionable bag?

Georg Jensen

22, Gal. du Roi (B1)
Metro Gare Centrale
☎ 512 9688
Tue.-Sat. 10.30am-1.30pm
and 2.30-6.30pm.

Thierry Struvay is one of a vanishing breed who cultivate a love of beauty. In his studio in the Galeries Saint-Hubert, he has revived the craze for Georg Jensen jewellery. These creations of silver and precious stones have followed all the trends in modern art since 1904. From early 20th-century exoticism to the extreme purity of line of the end of the century, in his shop you'll find the most beautiful pieces from the last hundred years.

Sabine Herman

86, Rue Faider (B3)
Tram 81/82-Trinité
☎ 640 7253
Tue.-Sat. noon-6pm,
closed 15 July-15 Aug.

For 10 years Sabine Herman, who trained in Antwerp, has been making timeless pieces of gold jewellery. Apart from her best-selling earrings, in the form of a spiral decorated with a pearl,

you'll find some stunning solitaires, an 'Opium' necklace and many-stranded rings (from BF5,500). The less valuable creations by other craftspeople, such as Tiziana, use wood, silver and *pâte de verre* in some marvellous pieces (from BF500).

Christa Reniers

29, Rue A.-Dansaert (A1)
☎ 514 1773
Mon.-Sat. 11am-6pm.

Globe artichokes, anemones, ears of corn, leaves, meteors and the sun, all carved in wax before being cast in heavy silver or gold. Shapes with a simple beauty and perfect balance

that can be worn as pendants, earrings or rings.

Laurent David

234, Gal. de la Porte-Louise (B2)
Metro Louise
☎ 511 2891
Mon.-Sat. 10am-6pm.

Bags in original, contemporary styles using only PVC as a matter of principle, to make the prices more accessible and enable women to carry beautiful accessories that don't cost a fortune. Imitation snakeskin and leather in unusual colour combinations such as blue and cognac or vermillion and yellow, or in the classic black and brown of the checked linings with their very English look. Travel bags at BF2,000; handbags from BF1,399.

Mulburry Company

12, Rue Jean-Stas (B2)
Metro Louise
☎ 537 7034
Mon.-Sat. 10am-6.30pm.

Indispensable accessories with a very British look for games of golf or Sundays in the country. For ladies, a real leather bag printed with a crocodile-skin pattern in lavender or pale yellow and an imitation leather personal organiser. For the gentlemen,

HOW TO GIVE YOUR SILVER JEWELLERY BACK ITS SHINE

Lay out your jewellery on a piece of aluminium foil in a glass bowl. Sprinkle it with salt, pour on boiling water and let it stand for a few minutes. The result is absolutely amazing, and you don't have to do any rubbing!

a very smart toilet bag, a small bag for golf balls and tees or a lizard-skin wallet. You pay for the name, of course: BF20,000 for a bag and BF10,000 for a toilet bag!

Timeless

142A, Av. Louise (B/C3)
Tram 94-Defacqz
☎ 648 4552
Tue.-Fri. 1.30-7pm.

Very valuable and expensive jewellery. A fine range of 20th-century gold and silver pieces and costume jewellery, with many Art Nouveau and Art Deco pieces as well as contemporary Scandinavian designs. Also among the treasures you'll find beautiful bags and scarves.

Italian Glove Shop

3, Gal. de la Reine (B1)
Metro Gare Centrale
☎ 512 7538
Mon.-Sat. 10am-12.30pm
and 1.30-6pm,
closed Mon. May to Sep.

Founded in 1890, this is one of those old-fashioned shops where you feel like lingering and trying on loads of gloves just for the pleasure of seeing the pairs in hand-stitched peccary skin, kid, silk-lined lambskin and sheepskin emerging from the drawers. It'll certainly put

you off all those woollen gloves you get in department stores. A pair from here is BF2,000 on average. Peccary skin is rarer and therefore more expensive.

Delvaux

27, Bd de Waterloo (B2)
Metro Louise
31, Gal. de la Reine (B1)
Metro Gare Centrale
☎ 513 0502
Mon.-Sat. 10am-6.30pm.

True excellence from this company, who have been producing bags made entirely by hand since 1829, including all fastenings and metal buckles. Besides their enormous creativity (30 to 40 new styles every year), Delvaux designs a multitude of accessories, from key-rings to motorcycle helmets, covered in tawny leather to match the silk scarves.

BRIC-A-BRAC, COLLECTIBLES AND FURNITURE

Hunting through the bric-a-brac stalls is the great weekend activity in Brussels. Rather than the flea market on Place du Jeu-de-Balle, which isn't very good on a Sunday, try the many junk shops and bric-a-brac sellers on Rue Blaes, Rue Haute and at the lower end of Sablon. To help you find the best antique shops, here are a few of the shops we recommend.

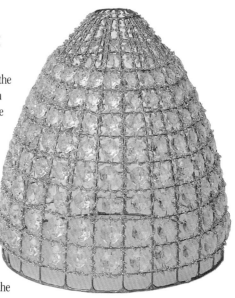

Collectors Gallery

17, Rue Lebeau (B2)
Bus 48-Grand-Sablon
☎ **511 4613**
Fri.-Sat. 11.30am-1.30pm
and 2.30-6pm, Sun.
11.30am-1.30pm
(ring to enter).

This is the perfect place for collectors! Valuable perfume bottles from The 1920s to the 1950s, old toys, Barbie dolls, mannequins and advertising artefacts await the connoisseur. For others this shop provides an opportunity to unearth an unusual object or a charming old dressing-table with movable mirrors.

Baden Baden

78-84, Rue Haute (A2)
Bus 20 and 48-Chapelle
☎ **548 9696**
Mon.-Sat.
10am-6.30pm
and Sun. 10am-
4pm.

Here you'll find early 20th-century bathroom ware and furniture in pale wood to give your modern bathroom an old-fashioned touch. This is just the place to find a traditional cast-iron bath tub with lions' paws for feet (BF65,000) or a beautiful porcelain sink.

Côte à Côte

2, Rue du Prévôt (B3)
Bus 54-Trinité
☎ **537 3304**
Mon.-Sat. 11am-6.30pm.

The furniture and other objects are just like this shop's lovely tiled floor, a little faded and out of fashion. Entire trousseaus with linen tablecloths, embroidered sheets and linen handkerchiefs, bath towels from an Italian grand hotel, an airman's headgear, horn-handled cutlery, old thermos flasks and a large leather suitcase to take all your treasures home with you.

Les Caves de Colette

59, Rue des Minimes (B2)
Bus 48-Grand-Sablon
☎ **511 7783**
Tue.-Thu.
noon-2pm,
Fri. and Sat.
11am-6pm,
Sun. 11am-1pm
or by appt.

Vases full of flowers, books lying on the table, a steaming cup of coffee... You feel as though you've been spirited into Colette's home. In fact you have, as she lives in this vast, light-filled cellar furnished with items she's picked up from around the world. As she loves a change of scene, it's all for sale, even the bed. An very unusual bric-a-brac shop full of still life paintings, pretty painted furniture and an odd assortment of crockery at modest prices.

Historic Marine

39A Rue des Lombards (A1)
Bus 48-Saint-Jean
☎ **513 8155**
Tue.-Sat 10.30am-7pm,
Sun. noon-6pm.

This shop, full of items rescued from yachts and liners and nautical weapons and instruments from the 18th century to the present day, is a favourite haunt of collectors of maritime antiques. The range of both goods and prices is extremely wide, not to mention the superb model boats. There's something here for any would-be sailor.

Curiosités

24, Rue du Chevreuil (A2)
Bus 20 and 48-Jeu-de-Balle
☎ **343 4811**
Tue.-Sun. 9am-2pm.

A real old-fashioned curiosity shop like something out of a Dickens novel. Old scientific instruments, a table football game from 1920, magic lanterns, clockwork toys and a roulette table alongside a 100x life-size reproduction of the human eye, an anatomical cross-section of a grasshopper and a viper in formaldehyde. Unique and rare objects all jumbled up in a tiny space that it's hard to tear yourself away from.

Papiers d'Antan

19, Rue de l'Hôpital (B1/2)
Bus 48-St-Jean
☎ **511 2470**
Tue.-Fri. 1.30-6pm,
Sat. 10am-6pm.

Posters, prints, old share certificates, menus, sheet music, magazines, postcards, religious pictures and old iron chests. Things to please any paper lovers who aren't interested in the latest

news – the most recent document here dates from 1950.

BARGAIN-HUNTING ON A SUNDAY

Apart from Place du Jeu-de-Balle and Sablon, here are a few other places for would-be bargain-hunters.
Rue Ropsy-Chaudron-Anderlecht (A2)
Bus 20-Abattoirs 7am-1pm. In the big hall of the livestock market.
Rue Vanderkindere and La Bascule-Uccle (HP)
Bus 38-Bascule. 7.30am-2pm.
Place Saint Denis-Forest (HP) Bus 50-St-Denis. 8am-1pm. Also, on the first Sunday of the month, the smartest bric-a-brac market in Brussels:
Place Saint-Lambert-Woluwé St-Lambert (D2)
Bus 80-Voot. 7am-1pm. To find out if and where any occasional bric-a-brac markets are being held, check the Saturday edition of the newspaper Le Soir.

OBJECTS FROM AROUND THE WORLD

If, on your travels, you've ever dreamed of bringing home a traditional Korean cabinet, the gates of a fallen rajah's palace, an enormous Chinese jar or a *zellije* tray, the objects of all your wildest dreams are gathered

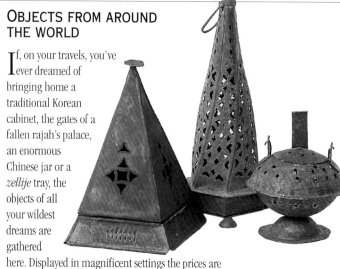

here. Displayed in magnificent settings the prices are quite derisory if you take account of the quality of the craftsmanship and the transportation costs.

Rambagh

64-70, Rue Haute (A2)
Bus 48-Chapelle
☎ 514 5827
Mon.-Sat. 10am-6.30pm
and Sun. 10am-3pm.

This shop is a true delight, filled with a wonderful collection of objects, in particular from Southeast Asia. The most extraordinary thing is that all the wonderful things you'll find here (wooden columns, varnished jars, Indian hammocks, Chinese beds, gargoyles, marble basins, candlesticks) are for sale. And at truly modest prices too.

Chinasty

8, Rue E.-Allard (B2)
Bus 48-Grand-Sablon
☎ 512 2301
Tue.-Fri. 1-6pm, Sat.
and Sun. 11am-6pm.

Traditional furniture from the depths of the Chinese countryside, restored and occasionally adapted to the requirements of life in Europe. Their purity of line is not unlike that of contemporary design and the wedding cupboards, consoles and low tables in natural or lacquered elm are no more expensive than furniture from Ikea. At these prices, why deprive yourself?

Le Jardin de Julie

214 Bis, Chaussée de Wavre
(B2/C2)
Bus 34/80-Trône
Tue.-Sat. 10am-6pm.

The Tuscan ceramics of Impruneta, the Rolls Royce of garden pottery, in different shapes and sizes: from large pots with garlands, *jardinières* and round pots with cherubs. The items are characteristically resistant to frost and comparatively highly priced (BF3,500), but they're worth it as a long-term investment. There are also lovely and less expensive ceramics from Florence and Siena decorated with glazed lemons. (BF2,280) and a wide range of 19th-century-style lamps by Maxime Pradier.

Alizari

13, Rue du Lombard (A/B3)
Bus 48-Plattesteen
Mon.-Sat. 11am-7pm

The range of Indian jewellery on offer in this neo-hippy-style shop is truly exceptional. There are period pieces to wear or collect as well as more recent creations at very reasonable prices (rings from BF300, necklaces at BF2,000). You'll also find large rugs set with mirrors (BF10,000) and buffalo hide bags made in Nepal.

Patio Céramiques

23-25-27, Rue des Chandeliers (B2)
Bus 48-Grand-Sablon
☎ 513 0313
Sat. 10am-6pm and Sun. 10am-2pm and by appt.

In a narrow street in Marolles you'll find all the peace and calm of a beautiful patio decorated with Moroccan *zelliges*, broken only by the gentle trickle of a fountain. Wonderful designs using ceramic tiles from Portugal, Morocco and Tunisia at BF70-200 a piece, or buy authentic *jobbana* (jars to

contain fat) and *khabia* (earthenware jars) from Fez.

Nuhr Nebi

23, Rue Blaes (B2)
Bus 48-Chapelle

☎ 514 0717
Tue.-Thu. 10am-6pm and Sat.-Sun. 11am-7pm.

A wide range of lamps and shelf units in wrought iron alongside kilims, Indonesian cupboards with drawers, Afghan chests and Tuareg jewellery. There are real finds here, like the magnificent Baroque glass balls (BF99-450) and Tibetan chess boards made of horn and ebony (BF2,500).

Imanza

50, Rue Van Artevelde (A1)
Metro Bourse
☎ 512 0636
Mon.-Sat. 10.30am-7pm.

This shop sells items from the Berber cultures of the Maghreb and the Arab cultures of India and Indonesia and is overflowing with period pottery, ethnic jewellery, lamps and craft items. The two Berber women who run it also offer you tea and sweetmeats, served in a tent in the basement. There is a wide range of CDs and specialist magazines and the chance to have designs painted in henna on your hands and feet.

Old and New Trading

7a, Quai du Bois-à-Construction (A1)
Metro Sainte-Catherine
☎ 219 4292
Sat.-Sun. 10.30am-6.30pm.

A jumble of furniture and objects from Indonesia, Rajasthan, Morocco and Iran. Just the place to find Planteur armchairs at good prices, a wardrobe in the Dutch colonial style or a teak divan. Equally beautiful are the ikaté fabrics, the wrought-iron wall lights, the ground glass crockery and a thousand and one other wonders.

TEAK, LOOK FOR THE GREEN LABEL

In recent years this hardwood, which has the characteristic of being impervious to rot, has acquired a popularity that may well cause the end of it. The indiscriminate felling of the forests of Asia, which are not yet protected by regulations, threatens the survival of the species. So, before you buy a piece of teak furniture, check where the wood comes from. If it isn't old wood that's been reused it must show the green label that guarantees it's from a properly-managed plantation..

Nightlife
Practicalities

Brussels has long had a reputation as a city that hosts performances of a wide range of interesting music at affordable prices and with good audiences. All the more reason to go to one of the large number of concerts – many of which are previews – and other events you'll find on offer all year round.

WHERE TO GO

You'll find the highest concentration of cafés, restaurants and trendy clubs near the Grand-Place, around Place Saint-Géry and La Bourse. This is where you should go if you want to have a drink or dance, particularly if you don't have transport. Sablon is another very lively area (full of the young and smart) in the early evening, particularly in summer. 'Matonge', the 'Congolese' quarter near Porte de Namur, echoes to the tropical rhythms of drums late into the night. There's always plenty of atmosphere in the bars, where the immaculately-dressed locals go to have a few *mukumbusu* (beers) in the company of their *londo* (fiancées). Meanwhile the big concert halls (the Palais des Beaux-Arts and Théâtre de la Monnaie) can easily be reached either on foot or by metro, but if you want to see some avant-garde theatre or cabaret in one of the various small venues scattered all over the city, you'll need to go by car, as public transport comes to a halt at midnight.

CLUBS

To put your finger on the pulse and find out where to go to party all night, call in at *Pitt's* or the *Pablo Disco Bar*, or pick up one of the flyers in the shop called *Prive Joke* (see p. 85). The trendy bars, an indispensable port of call before the scene hits the clubs on a Saturday night, are also busy in the week with drinkers who go for the sounds and to check out the local DJs. The clubs open their doors at 11pm, but they're totally deserted before 12.30 or 1am. If you haven't got a membership card and you aren't going with a member, make sure you're familiar with the dress code, which may be fancy, techno or high fashion, but is always original. Prices vary from night to night and club to club, though they're always higher on Saturday night (BF200-500). To find out more about partying all night call ☎ 534 2392. These people will fill you in on all the latest gossip and give you the names of the hottest and coolest clubs in and around the city.

HOW TO BOOK TICKETS

To book a seat for the theatre or ballet from abroad, call the box office at the venue directly and they'll send you your tickets (a credit card is indispensable). For very popular performances it's a good idea to book in advance to be sure of getting a seat. Once you're in Brussels, the receptionist at your hotel can book your tickets for you, or else you can get them from the tourist office.

TIB: Brussels Town Hall-Grand-Place
Open every day 9am-6pm.

OPT: 63, Rue du Marché-aux-Herbes
Open 1 Nov-30 April, Mon.-Fri. 9am-6pm, Sat. 9am-1pm, 2-6pm, Sun. 9am-1pm, 1 May-31 Oct. same times except Sun. 9am-1pm, 2-6pm.

You can always try your luck at the last minute by going to the venue of your choice one hour before the performance starts.

CAFÉS

From the everyday charm of the wood-pannelled local, to the trendy place-to-be-seen, with designer decor and over-the-shoulder glances, and from noisy cabaret venues to 'brown cafés' with walls veneered by generations of smokers, the denizens of Brussels love their cafés and spend a good part of their lives in them. Cafés open around 8am, close at 1am in the week, 2-3am at weekends, and have a very mixed clientele. The young go to old people's cafés and you'll see drinkers in their fifties in the trendiest places and bisexuals in the gay bars. All have one thing in common: they drink a lot of strong beer and enjoy being out in a crowd.

WHAT TO WEAR

If you're intending to spend an evening out at the opera, eating in a star-rated restaurant or even listening to a concert at the Palais des Beaux-Arts, don't forget to include your evening dress or smart suit and tie in your luggage. On the other hand, dressing smartly can be a problem if you want to get into some of the clubs, such as the *Mirano*, which have a very strict dress code. These range from designer labels to alternative dressing – the thing is to know which, and remember – it's the detail that matters.

PERSONAL SAFETY

Brussels isn't generally a dangerous place, by day or by night. Of course, like other big cities, it has its share of pickpockets, who operate in the metro and other crowded places, but if you use a little common-sense, you shouldn't have any trouble. All the same, if you're on foot, it's a good idea to avoid passing through Place Anneessens late at night, and the same goes for the areas around the Gare du Nord and the Gare du Midi stations.

CULTURAL CALENDAR

To help you plan your stay, try and get hold of the monthly magazine *Kiosque*, which is on sale in Belgian bookshops (or write to 119, Avenue Coghen-1180 Bruxelles; website: www.exmachina.be/kiosque). This gives you the best information on forth-coming events of every kind, the most fashionable bars and restaurants and the hippest clubs, along with some amusing short articles. You can also buy the monthly magazine *Park-Mail Pocket* in bookshops. The newspaper *Le Soir* has a supplement called 'MAD' on Wednes-days, which carries the full programme of the week's cultural events. You'll also find a few pages of listings on Fridays (except in July and August) in the daily newspaper *La Libre Belgique*. Complete listings of the week's events can be found in the English-language weekly magazine, *The Bulletin*, which comes out on Wednesdays. Lastly, the weekly calendar *BBB* is available at the tourist office in Grand-Place.

CONCERTS, THEATRE, OPERA, DANCE AND CABARET

Palais des Beaux-Arts

23, Rue Ravenstein (B1)
Metro Gare Centrale
☎ 507 8200
Box office open. Mon.-Sat.
11am-6pm or tel. bookings
Mon.-Fri. 9am-7pm and
Sat. 9am-6pm.
Seats from BF450.

All concerts start at 8pm. This building, which was designed by Victor Horta, is home to the Brussels Philharmonic Society, which stages concerts of orchestral music all year round as well as recitals, chamber music and early and contemporary music during the Ars Musica festival. Most of the concerts are performed by the Belgian National Orchestra, but internationally renowned artists and young musicians of proven talent also perform here. In May every three out of four years (violin, piano and singing) the building is the venue for the prestigious Queen Elisabeth Competition. Exhibitions and dance and theatre performances can also be seen here.

Theatre Royal de la Monnaie

Pl. de la Monnaie (B1)
Metro De Brouckère
☎ 229 1211
BF300-3,700.

The reputation of Belgium's finest opera house has spread abroad, to the point where it's easier for a foreigner to book a seat from a booking centre than it is for a Brussels' inhabitant who isn't on the mailing list. As well as opera, it also hosts concerts and ballet performances.

Hotel Astoria

103, Rue Royale (B1)
Bus 29-63-Congrès
☎ 513 0965
Booking Mon.-Sat.
9am-6.30pm
Seats BF250.

The Venetian chandeliers and gilded mirrors of the Waldorf room in one of the city's grand hotels of the Belle Époque provide the setting for concerts of chamber music every Sunday at 11am.

St Michel's Cathedral

Parvis Sainte-Gudule (B1)
Metro Gare Centrale
☎ 217 8345.

Every Sunday at 10am there's a mass with plainsong sung in the Gothic cathedral by the Gregorian Scola and conducted by Michel Huybrechts.

Brigittines Chapel

1, Rue des Visitandines (B2)
Bus 48-Sablon
☎ 279 6443.

A fine Baroque chapel near Sablon, which has been converted into a performance space for concerts, theatre and ballet.

Church of Sts-Jean-et-Étienne-aux-Minimes

62, Rue des Minimes (B2)
Bus 48-Sablon
☎ 511 9384
Mon.-Fri. 10am-noon.

Besides a plainsong mass every Sunday at 11.30am, this collegiate church, with its superb organs, hosts free concerts of Bach, Mendelsohn or Handel every other Sunday from April to November at 4pm (3pm in July and August). Other classical music concerts, particularly during Sablon's Baroque spring festival in April, are performed on weekday evenings at 8pm.

Royal Circus

81, Rue de l'Enseignement (C1)
Metro Madou
☎ 218 2015.

In 1953 the Circus, built in 1879, was converted into a venue for performances of every kind: concerts, operas, dance, variety, revues and of course circus shows.

Botanique

236, Rue Royale (B1)
Metro Botanique
☎ **226 1211.**

The French community housed in the prestigious setting of the old orangeries and tropical greenhouses stages concerts, films and various festivals which are always at the cutting edge of the multicultural arts.

Halles de Schaerbeek

22A, Rue Royale-Sainte-Marie (HP)
Tram 92-Place de la Reine
☎ **227 5960.**

This glass and iron structure, one of the last vestiges of 19th-century industrial architecture, has become a very trendy multimedia cultural centre hosting a hip-hop festival, world music and dance.

National Theatre

Pl. Rogier (B1)
Metro Rogier
☎ **203 5303**
Booking Tue.-Sat. 11am-6pm.

Comedy, satire and tragedy are all performed here. Excellent productions of classic plays.

Theatre 140

140, Av. Plasky (D1)
Bus 29-63-Plasky
☎ **733 9708.**

This sis the place to come to see avant-garde plays and dance performances, plus a wide range of cabaret acts and concerts. A venue you can depend on for a good evening out.

Theatre Toone

6, Impasse Schuddeveld-Petite Rue des Bouchers (A1)
Metro Bourse
☎ **513 5486**
Performances at 8.30pm from Tue. to Sat.

The classics are performed here by puppets, speaking in the Brussels' dialect.

Theatre de la Balsamine

1, Av. Félix Marchal (D1)
Bus 29-Dailly
☎ **735 6468.**

A venue where you can see plays and choreography by young rising stars and foreign artists. It also stages an annual dance festival and performances of shadow plays.

Theatre Varia

78, Rue du Sceptre (C2)
Bus 95-96-Blyckaerts
☎ **640 8258.**

Avant-garde theatre and dance performances.

Espace Senghor

366, Chaussée de Wavre (C2/D3)
Bus 59-80-Jourdan
☎ **230 2988**
Box office Mon. and Thu. noon-2pm and 4-6pm.

This showcase for world music and non-Western culture hosts theatre and dance performances and concerts.

Fool Moon

28, Quai de Mariemont (HP)
Bus 20-89-Birmingham
☎ **410 1003.**

Around 10pm there's live music from around the world: salsa, pop, hip-hop, Senegalese musci, funk, soul and the odd bit of rock. A noisy crowd swarms in after midnight, but you can still relax on a sofa upstairs and chat.

Ancienne Belgique

110, Bd Anspach (A1)
Metro Bourse
☎ 548 2424.

The main venue for good pop and rock concerts. Well worth a visit one night.

Chez Flo

25, Rue au Beurre (A1)
Metro Bourse
☎ 513 3152
Wed.-Sun. from 8pm; show from 9.30pm.

One of the absolute musts of nightlife in Brussels for people who like to watch a show during dinner. You'll be provided with a drag show on stage and good French cuisine on the table. It's best to book in advance to get a table with a good view.

In addition, from July to the end of August, there are free classical and jazz concerts on the English lawn of La Cambre every Sunday morning at 11am, the Bellone-Brigittines festival in mid-August hosts performances of contemporary dance, music and theatre, and the festivals of Wallonia (July) and Flanders (August) offer music-lovers a plethora of concerts.

Jazz clubs and live music

Many cafés – and some restaurants – that stay open until 3am have live music, particularly on Friday and Saturday nights. You can also get a light meal until midnight or 1am. In addition to the excellent programmes of the jazz clubs, there's a jazz marathon (last weekend in May) every year in most of the cafés, and in mid-July the open air theatre below the Atomium echoes to the sounds of folk and jazz for a whole weekend.

Travers

11, Rue Traversière (B1)
Metro Botanique
☎ 218 4086.

An unpretentious little venue in an odd area that's packed with connoisseurs of good, intimate-style jazz and experimental music. Concerts or jam sessions every night (except Sundays).

Sounds

28, Rue de la Tulipe (B2)
Metro Porte de Namur
☎ 512 9250.

A little café with live music patronised by jazz-lovers and, once a week, fans of the tango and Latino jam session.

Le Cercle

20-22 Rue Saint-Anne (B2)
☎ 514 0353
Nightly, perf. at 8.30pm.

A theatre-café near Place du Sablon, which stages a jam session on Tuesdays, French chanson as well as singers from other countries on Wednesdays and Thursdays, Afro-Cuban music on Fridays and then a disco on Saturdays. Not forgetting the philosophy afternoons on Sundays and the plays on Mondays!

The Bank

79, Rue du Bailli (B3)
Bus 54, trams 81-82-Trinité
☎ 537 5265.

THE BANK
IRISH PUB

Sharon Farren

Rue du Bailli 79
1050 Bruxelles
Tel: 0032-2-5375265
Fax: 0032-2-5373724
TVA: 554493253

Irish and cosy by day, but hot and crowded at night. Every Thursday and Saturday night from 10pm they bring the house down with rock or Irish music. The toilets are down in the bank's strongroom, which is protected by a double armour-plated door!

Grain d'Orge

142, Chaussée de Wavre (B2)
Metro Porte de Namur
☎ 511 2647.

A 'brown café' where generations of young have worn the wooden seats smooth while they drink the strong beer. Free blues, rock and rhythm and blues concerts every Friday at 9.30pm (except in summer).

Marcus Jazz Spot

4, Impasse de la Fidélité,
Rue de la Fourche (B1)
☎ 502 0297
Mon.-Sat. 8pm-3am.

A trendy modern jazz café-restaurant in a cul-de-sac off the well-known Rue des Bouchers. Six concerts a week, including a jam session on Wed. from 9pm.

Tierra del Fuego

14, Rue Berckmans (B2)
☎ 537 4272
Every night 7pm-1 or 2am.

A bar-restaurant with a slightly oriental decor by Paul Parker and a lovely Gaudi-style garden. This is the meeting place of the Brussels' Latinos, who dance to bossa nova and salsa while smoking large, aromatic Havana cigars. Some live music, theme nights and a dish of the day at BF200.

Thunderbird

48, Quai du Commerce-(HP)
Metro Yser
☎ 219 3980.

Next-door to a snooker school, this is a new Flemish café-restaurant where they serve tex-mex with a background of live blues and country music (Fridays and Saturdays at 10pm).

La Movida

3, Rue Saint-Géry (A1)
Metro Bourse
☎ 502 0284
From 9pm, closed Mon.

Hot Andalucian nights in the heart of Brussels: *tapas* every night and flamenco at weekends, enjoyed by the mainly Spanish-

speaking audience. Less lively during the week when karaoke is on offer instead.

O Novo Brasil

88, Rue de la Caserne (A2)
Metro Lemonnier
☎ 513 5028
Fri. and Sat. 7pm-5am.

A lovely vaulted cellar which echoes to the rhythmic sounds of the bossa nova, played by highly skilled musicians. Here you can dance until dawn getting drunk on Caipirinha, or eat exotic food from 7pm. There's a Cuban evening once a month when you can let your hair down to the sounds of salsa.

Bazaar

63, Rue des Capucins (A2)
Bus 48-Chapelle
☎ 511 2600
7.30pm-1am, closed Mon.

An ex-secondhand clothes dealer has displayed some old hangings as a kind of hot-air balloon over the bar, hung some

flecked mirrors on the wall and arranged an assortment of old armchairs around a dimly-lit warehouse – a formula that has had Brussels under its spell for a while now. Before you get in, expect to queue for a long time in the street and then pay BF150 membership fee. When you're at last allowed in, you may be able to listen to a concert of world music (for which there is another charge). At least you know that you are in one of Belgium's trendiest bars. Belgian-Mediterranean cuisine is also available, but it's overpriced.

Cafés

À Malte

30, Rue Berckmans (B2)
Metro Louise
☎ 537 0991.

All day long people drop in here for breakfast, brunch, tea, an aperitif or a long late-night chat by candlelight. There are little notes stuck all over the walls, deep leather armchairs in which you can read the old books lying around on the shelves, a wooden mezzanine floor that hangs like a cradle, lamp stands made from teaspoons and Rakham the Red's treasure locked away in the aquarium bar – in other words a wonderful place you really must visit, both for the atmosphere and the decor. Just step inside and you'll see…

Zébra

33-35, Pl. Saint-Géry (A1)
Metro Bourse
☎ 511 0901
Open daily noon-1.30am.

A large, sunny terrace that is always full in summer, ethnic music in the evenings, salad and *focaccia* any time, and reasonable prices. A varied and cosmopolitan crowd like to hang out here.

Les Salons de l'Atalaïde

89, Chaussée de Charleroi (B2)
Metro Louise
☎ 537 2154
Every day noon-midnight.

The city's wildest interior. A vast mansion whose rooms each have a different mood. There's the Arab-Indian room with furniture from Rajasthan, the private room hung with Cordoba leather, the first floor terrace, the flying carpet hanging from the ceiling, the paintings by a Brazilian artist, the marble staircase and the Babylonian gate. Sadly the food isn't really up to scratch, but you can just stop by for a drink.

L'Amour Fou

185, Chaussée d'Ixelles (B2/C3)
Bus 71-F. Cocq
☎ 514 2709
9-2 or 3am (10am at weekends).

The interior has had a total makeover for a more intimate atmosphere, a real local bar with newspapers for the clients (aged 18-30), where you can eat at any time. A local institution.

P.P. Café

28, Rue Van Praet (B1)
Metro De Brouckére
☎ 514 2562
Open daily noon-2.30pm.

The wild foyer of the Pathé Palace, a well-known cinema of the 1920s and 30s, has regained its old magnificence to become *the* 'stamcafé' for the area's trend-setters. Mirrors, columns, flowery frescoes and gorgons smile beneath their gold leaf. Unpretentious light meals.

Le Soleil

86, Rue du Marché-au-Charbon (A1)
Metro Bourse
☎ 513 3430
Mon.-Sat. 10am-1pm (2pm Fri. and Sat.), Sun. 11-1am.

This is a real old-fashioned café with wood panelling that brought new life to the entire area when it re-opened back in

1990. A background of jazz or dance music, tables and chairs sprawling across the pedestrianised street and a friendly clientele aged mostly between 20 and 40.

Pablo Disco bar

60, Rue du Marché-au-Charbon (A1)
Metro Bourse
☎ 514 5149
Open every day from 8pm, closed Sun. and Mon. in winter.

This Latino-style bar, with red imitation leather seats and a blue and yellow courtyard, is the ideal place to start or end your night. A DJ brings in the house and acid jazz fans every evening. Best not to overdo the *pablito* cocktail served in a shaker or the little glass of ice-cold spirits known as a *chupito*.

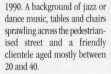

Bars

Java

31, Rue Saint-Géry (A1)
Metro Bourse
☎ 512 3716
Mon.-Thu. 6pm-2am, Fri.-Sat. 6pm-4.30 or 5am.

This small, lively local bar, with a decor inspired by Gaudi, is patronised by French speakers who come in for cocktails and all kinds of beers. There's great music, some of it live, and a buzzing atmosphere.

city's first anti-interior design bar, whose decor is the work of two film set designers. King Leopold II has a prime position from which to contemplate his cosmopolitan subjects as they enjoy a few drinks.

Bizon

7, Rue du Pont-de-la-Carpe (A1)
Metro Bourse
☎ 502 4699
From 8pm-3am.

A small saloon bar serving cheap beers watched over by the bison head on the wall. There's live blues-style music on Thursdays.

Dali's bar

35, Petite Rue des Bouchers (A1)
Metro Bourse
☎ 511 5467
From 10pm till dawn, closed Sun.

A long midnight-blue corridor leads to the Surrealist fantasies of Salvador Dali: you'll find soft watches dripping down the bar and sofas shaped like full-lipped mouths along with other meta-morphoses. You sit surrounded by art to sip cocktails at neo-realist prices and listen to the DJ's selection, from the hits of the 1960s to house music.

Acrobat

14-16, Rue Borgval (A1)
Metro Bourse
☎ 513 7308
Tue.-Sat. after 10pm, until 5am at weekends.

One of the best places in down-town Brussels to have a drink or dance to the groovy funk sounds. A mixed and generally fairly young crowd on the dance-floor. There are bouncers on the door, but you don't have to pay to get in here.

Archiduc

6, Rue Antoine-Dansaert (A1)
Metro Bourse
☎ 512 0652
Open every day after 4pm.

A very smart Art Deco piano-bar with a somewhat stuffy clientele who sip their whiskies with a background of jazz music, sometimes played live. The place has been a Brussels' institution since 1937.

Belgica

32, Rue du Marché-au-Charbon (A1)
Metro Bourse
Thu.-Sun. 10pm-3am.

With its stripped wallpaper and minimalist furniture, this is the

Le Sud

43, Rue de l'Ecuyer (B1)
Metro De Brouckère
Thu.-Sat. 10pm-3am (6am at weekends).

Different atmospheres on diffe-rent sides of the bar, concerts and theme nights for young grunge and underground types.

Beursschouwburg

20-28 Rue A.-Orts (A/B1)
☎ 513 8290
Thu.-Sat. 9pm-3am to 5am, performances at 8.30/10pm.

The Beursschouwburg has many faces, hosting performances of ethnic music, avant-garde theatre and all different kinds of music-related events. After midnight at the steel and brick bar you can enjoy a drink with a crowd of intellectuals and trendy young multilingual Flemish people.

Tom Tom Club

5, Pl. de la Constitution (A2)
Metro Lemonnier
☎ 523 2369
Open every night 7pm-1am.

A breath of salsa and funk blows over this lovely old early 20th-century café, now converted into a bar and dancefloor where everyone's out to enjoy them-selves. Much frequented by Mediterranean types. Tea dances every Sunday.

Coaster

28, Rue des Riches-Claires (A1)
☎ 512 0847
Open every night 8pm-5am or 8am.

A superb copper bar and acid jazz ambiance for connoisseurs of whisky (60 sorts) and vodka (40 brands). Chat during the happy hours from 8-11pm and dance till dawn at the weekend.

Le Courant d'Alcyon

80A, Rue Brogniez (A2)
Metro Midi
Thu and Fri. at 9pm
(ring to enter).

At this highly confidential address, defining itself as a contemporary bar and night gallery, there are screenings of short and experimental films

and videos, some with live performances. There's dancing in the basement and debates upstairs. It's all a bit mysterious but located fairly and squarely in the twenty-first century.

Clubs

Fuse

208, Rue Blaes (B2)
Open Sat.

This new club in the heart of Marolles is where the young go for techno music mixed by the best DJs from Europe and the USA. A great many theme nights and live performances publicised by flyers.

Mirano

38, Chaussée de Louvain (C/D1)
Open Sat.

For some years now this former cinema has been *the* trendy club to be seen in some time during

the night. Revellers are both young and not-so-young, mainly working in film, fashion or advertising. The 'Mir' doorman is extremly fussy where style is concerned, so don't bother trying to get in unless you are dressed in the latest fashions.

The Sparrow

16, Rue Duquesnoy (B1)
☎ 512 6622
Thu.-Sat. from 11pm.

Just by Grand-Place, the former *Garage* club has had a total makeover. Hip soul music, theme nights, disco on Thursdays and salsa on Saturdays. While it was once an exclusively gay club, it now has a more mixed clientele.

Fool Moon

26, Quai de Mariemont (HP)
☎ 410 1003
Fri. and Sat. after 9pm.

By the canal in a rather more seedy part of the city, this club hosts performances of ethnic music and raves where they play jazz, hip-hop, funk, groove, you name it, they'll play it.

Chez Johnny (At the Claridge)

24, Chaussée de Louvain (C/D1)
☎ 227 3999
Fri. and Sat. after 11pm.

Something of the village dance hall and reminiscent of the good old days. Nostalgic thirty-somethings and more youthful types rub shoulders after getting their hands stamped at the door.

Jeux d'Hiver

Bois de La Cambre (HP)
☎ 649 0864
Thu, Fri. and Sat.

All the hits are played at this club for the offspring of the well-heeled Uccle residents, who drive

up in their Porsches and BMWs. Even if you aren't one of them, you really should visit at least once in your lifetime.

AN EVENING WALK

Brussels is not a city where people go for a stroll on a winter's evening, but as soon as the temperature rises above 18°C/66°F, the restaurants and bars overflow onto the pavement, the streets start to bustle, there's a proliferation of shows and concerts and, if the temperature drops again, there are a great many warm cafés to take refuge in.

SABLON

Begin your walk in Place du Grand-Sablon, a lovely square lined with mansions and a fine Gothic church whose stained-glass windows are lit up when night falls. Sitting at a table at the terrace of the *Grain de Sable* (15-16, Pl. du Grand-Sablon), you can have dinner or a drink as you watch the horse-drawn carriages amid the buzz of gossip and mobile phones. After a wander down the pedestrian street (Rollebeek), which is always very busy until at least

1am, return to the top of Sablon, leaving the church of Notre-Dame on your right. take a look towards the huge mass of the law courts, which block your view down the Rue de la Régence, before walking on to Place Royale, where Godefroy de Bouillon brandished the crusaders' standard.

PLACE ROYALE

This square with its arcades is marked by harmonious proportions and a sober style. Off of one corner you'll find the vast royal palace, overlooking a park where concerts are held in summer. Or, by going through the arcade that crosses Rue de Namur, you'll reach the African quarter of 'Matongé', where they're up late all year round.

From the square, take a short walk of 50 m/yds down Rue Montagne-de-la-Cour, to an esplanade from where you have a superb view of Grand-Place, marked by the jagged outline of the Town Hall's spire. In front of you there's a stairway through a garden laid out in a geometric design. This is surrounded by the Albertine, whose architecture is reminiscent of buildings erected by Mussolini, but seems a little less imposing at night. After crossing the boulevard guarded on either side by the statues of King Albert I and Queen Elisabeth, walk down the cobbled street of La Madeleine.

AROUND GRAND-PLACE

All roads lead to the illuminated Grand-Place. It's a magical sight despite all the hustle and bustle and every language is spoken on the café terraces. This is the time to pause once more for a glass of Trappiste beer, particularly if you've arrived in time for the *son et lumière*. Make sure you visit either *La Chaloupe d'Or* or *Le Roi d'Espagne*, two cafés housed in old corporation houses, with their wood-panelled interiors containing disparate collections of objects.

There's a free *son et lumière* show on Grand-Place every evening from the end of March to the end of September (10pm in April and August, 10.30pm from May to the end of July and 9.30pm in September).

Don't miss taking a walk down the Rue des Bouchers, which is literally packed with tourist restaurants, jugglers, jewellery sellers and musicians (watch out for pickpockets!). Make your way back to the illuminated Bourse, casting your eye into the café-bodega *Le Cirio*, where venerable old locals can be seen swigging beer night and day in a hispano-Flemish setting.

If you're not a great fan of bars and clubs, now's the time to take the last metro or bus back to your hotel.

DOWNTOWN

For night-owls the party's just beginning. The *tapas* bars, cafés where DJs spin the sounds, trendy restaurants where you can get a meal late into the night, dance-bars and clubs are all concentrated in the Rue du Marché-au-Charbon, the Rue Antoine- Dansaert and Place Saint-Géry.

Late night hunger pangs
Le Falstaff
17-25, Rue Henri-Maus (A1)
(near Bourse)

This magnificent café dating from 1883, which has sadly fallen victim to its own success, is still a good place to get a bite to eat at any time. It isn't very refined and the waiters tend to be on the grumpy side, but when hunger calls...

Night shops

What a good thing there are shops that stay open all night! Cigarettes, toothpaste, samosas, vegetables, they've got it all, and at prices that are only slightly higher than in the daytime supermarkets.

Bicycle tours by night
Provélo
15, Rue de Londres (B/C2)
☎ 502 7355.

Every Saturday evening at 7pm Provélo run different themed tours, stopping off in typical cafés (so it's a good idea to wear your helmet!).

Useful expressions – Flemish

USEFUL EXPRESSIONS

Yes/No: *Ja/Nee*
Hello: *Hallo*
Goodbye: *Goededag*
Please: *Alstublieft*
Thank you: *Dank U*
You're welcome: *Graag gedaan*
I don't speak Dutch/ Flemish: *Ik spreek geen Nederlands/Vlaams*
Do you speak English?: *Spreekt U Engels?*
I don't understand: *Ik begrijp het niet*
Could you repeat that, *Kunt u dat alstublieft herhalen?*
Pardon?: *Pardon?*
Excuse me: *Excuseert U mij*
How are you?: *Hoe gaat het?*
Very well, thank you: *Prima, dank U*
Pleased to meet you: *Het verheugd mij U te ontmoeten*
Who?: *Wie?*
Where?: *Waar?*
When?: *Wanneer?*
Why?: *Waarom?*
Which?: *Welke?*
good/bad: *goed/slecht*
big/small: *groot/klein*
hot/cold: *warm/koud*
open/closed: *open/gesloten*

AT THE HOTEL

I have a reservation: *Ik heb een reservatie*
Do you have any vacancies?: *Heeft U een onbezette kamer?*
How much is it?: *Hoeveel kost het?*
I would like…: *Graag wil ik ..*

a single room: *een eenpersoonskamer*
a room with double bed: *een tweepersoonskamer*
for one night: *voor één nacht*
for two nights: *voor twee nachten*
a quiet room: *een rustige kamer*
with a bathroom: *met badkamer*
with a shower: *met douche*
key: *sleutel*
1st floor: *eerste verdiep*
2nd floor: *tweede verdiep*
lift/elevator: *lift*

IN THE RESTAURANT

Do you have a table?: *Is er een tafel vrij?*
I would like to reserve a table: *Ik wil graag een tafel reserveren*
The menu please: *Het menu, alstublieft*
starter: *voorgerecht*
main course: *hoofdschotel*
dessert: *dessert*
breakfast: *ontbijt*
lunch: *middageten*
dinner: *diner*
The bill, please: *De rekening, alstublieft*
ashtray: *asbakje*
I am a vegetarian: *Ik ben vegetariër*
waiter: *kelner*
Is the service included?: *Is dienst inbegrepen?*
soup: *soep*
beef: *rundvlees*
lamb: *lamsvlees*
pork: *varkensvlees*
chicken: *kip*

duck: *eend*
fish: *vis*
vegetables: *groenten*
green salad: *sla*
chips/french fries: *frieten*
rare(steak): *kort gebakken*
medium: *middelmatig gebakken*
well done: *goed doorgebakken*
cheese: *kaas*
bread: *brood*
butter: *boter*
knife: *mes*
fork: *vork*
spoon: *lepel*
water: *water*
wine: *wijn*
beer: *bier*
coffee: *koffie*
milk: *melk*
bottle: *fles*
drink: *drank*

SHOPPING

How much is it?: *Hoeveel kost het?*
Do you have…?: *Heeft U…*
Do you accept credit cards?: *Aanvaard U kredietkaarten?*
cash: *contant*
I'm just looking: *Ik kijk wat rond*
department store: *grootwarenhuis*
supermarket: *supermarkt*
market: *markt*
antique shop: *antiquiteiten*
bank: *bank*
chemist/drugstore: *apotheker*
shoe shop: *schoenenwinkel*
post office: *postkantoor*
tobacconist: *sigarenwinkel*

IN THE TOWN

Where is/are?: *Waar is/zijn?*
map of the city: *kaart van de stad*
Is it far?: *Is het ver?*
Tourist information office: *Toeristkantoor*
church: *kerk*
cathedral: *kathedraal*
castle: *kasteel*
museum: *museum*
town hall: *stadshuis*
garden: *tuin*
art gallery: *kunstgalerie*
square: *plein*
street: *straat*
railway station: *spoorwegstation*
metro/underground: *metro (ondergrondse)*
tram: *tram*
taxi: *taxi*
bus: *bus*
ticket: *kaartje*
single/return: *enkeltje/retourtje*

NUMBERS

1 *Een*
2 *Twee*
3 *Drie*
4 *Vier*
5 *Vijf*
6 *Zes*
7 *Zeven*
8 *Acht*
9 *Negen*
10 *Tien*
20 *Twintig*
30 *Dertig*
40 *Veertig*
50 *Vijftig*
60 *Zestig*
70 *Zeventig*
80 *Tachtig*
90 *Negentig*
100 *Honderd*
1000 *Duizend*
Million *Miljoen*

Useful expressions – French

USEFUL EXPRESSIONS

Yes/No: *Oui/Non*
Good morning/Hello: *Bonjour*
Good evening/night: *Bonsoir*
Hello/Goodbye (very informal): *Salut*
Goodbye: *Au revoir*
Please: *S'il vous plaît*
Thank you: *Merci*
You're welcome: *De rien*
I don't speak French: *Je ne parle pas français*
Do you speak English?: *Parlez-vous anglais?*
I don't understand: *Je ne comprend pas*
Could you repeat that, please?: *Pouvez-vous répéter, s'il vous plaît?*
Pardon?: *Comment?*
Excuse me: *Excusez-moi*
How are you?: *Comment allez-vous?*
Very well, thank you: *Très bien, merci.*
Pleased to meet you: *Enchanté/Enchantée (m/f)*
Who?: *Qui?*
Where is?: *Où est?*
Where are?: *Où sont?*
When?: *Quand?*
Why?: *Pourquoi?*
Which?: *Quel (m)/ Quelle (f)?*
good: *bon*
bad: *mauvais*
big: *grand*
small: *petit*
hot: *chaud*
cold: *froid*
open: *ouvert*
closed: *fermé*

AT THE HOTEL

I have a reservation: *J'ai réservé…*
How much is it?: *C'est combien, s'il vous plaît?/Combien ça coute?*
I would like…: *Je voudrais…*
a single room: *une chambre à un lit pour une personne*
a room with double bed: *une chambre à un lit pour deux personnes*
for one night: *pour une nuit*
for two nights: *pour deux nuits*
a quiet room: *une chambre calme*
a room with a bathroom: *une chambre avec salle de bains*
with a shower: *avec douche*
key: *la clef*
1st/2nd floor etc: *premier/deuxième étage*
ground floor: *le rez-de-chaussée (RC)*
lift/elevator: *l'ascenseur*

IN THE RESTAURANT

Do you have a table?: *Avez-vous une table de libre?*
I would like to reserve a table: *Je voudrais réserver une table*
menu: *le menu/la carte*
starter: *l'entrée/le hors-d'oeuvre*
main course: *le plat principal*
dessert: *le dessert*
breakfast: *le petit dejeuner*
lunch: *le dejeuner*
dinner: *le dîner*
The bill, please: *L'addition, s'il-vous-plaît*
ashtray: *un cendrier*

I am a vegetarian: *Je suis végétarien(ne) (m/f)*
waiter: *Monsieur*
waitress: *Madame, Mademoiselle*
Is the service included?: *Est-ce que le service est compris?*
soup: *la soupe/le potage*
beef: *le boeuf*
lamb: *l'agneau*
pork: *le porc*
chicken: *le poulet*
duck: *le canard*
fish: *le poisson*
vegetables: *les légumes*
green salad: *une salade verte*
chips/french fries: *les frites*
very rare: *bleu*
rare: *saignant*
medium: *à point*
well done: *bien cuit*
cheese: *le fromage*
bread: *le pain*
butter: *le beurre*
knife: *le couteau*
fork: *la forchette*
spoon: *la cuillère*
some tap water: *de l'eau du robinet*
some mineral water: *de l'eau minérale*
red/white wine: *le vin rouge/blanc*
a beer: *une bière*
a coffee: *un café*
a coffee with milk: *un café au lait*
some milk: *du lait*
a bottle of: *une bouteille de*
a drink: *un boisson*

SHOPPING

How much is it, please?: *C'est combien, s'il vous plaît?*
Do you have…?: *Avez-vous…?*

Do you accept credit cards?: *Est-ce que vous acceptez les cartes de crédit?*
in cash: *en espèces*
I'm just looking, thank you: *Je regarde, merci.*
department store: *le grand magasin/la grande surface*
baker: *la boulangerie*
market: *le marché*
antique shop: *le magasin d'antiquités*
bank: *la banque*
delicatessen: *la charcuterie*
cake shop: *la pâtisserie*
chemist/drugstore: *la pharmacie*
shoe shop: *le magasin de chaussures*
post office: *la poste/le PTT*
tobacconist: *le tabac*

IN THE TOWN

map of the city: *un plan de la ville*
Is it far?: *C'est loin?*
tourist information office: *l'office de tourisme/ le syndicat d'initiative*
church: *l'église*
cathedral: *la cathédrale*
castle: *le château*
museum: *le musée*
town hall: *la mairie*
garden: *le jardin*
square: *la place*
street: *la rue*
railway station: *la gare*
bus station: *la gare routière*
the underground: *le métro*
underground station: *la station de métro*
ticket: *le billet*
single ticket: *un aller simple*
return ticket: *un aller-retour*

Conversion tables for clothes shopping

Women's sizes

Shirts/dresses

U.K	U.S.A	EUROPE
8	6	36
10	8	38
12	10	40
14	12	42
16	14	44
18	16	46

Sweaters

U.K	U.S.A	EUROPE
8	6	44
10	8	46
12	10	48
14	12	50
16	14	52

Shoes

U.K	U.S.A	EUROPE
3	5	36
4	6	37
5	7	38
6	8	39
7	9	40
8	10	41

Men's sizes

Shirts

U.K	U.S.A	EUROPE
14	14	36
$14^{1/2}$	$14^{1/2}$	37
15	15	38
$15^{1/2}$	$15^{1/2}$	39
16	16	41
$16^{1/2}$	$16^{1/2}$	42
17	17	43
$17^{1/2}$	$17^{1/2}$	44
18	18	46

Suits

U.K	U.S.A	EUROPE
36	36	46
38	38	48
40	40	50
42	42	52
44	44	54
46	46	56

Shoes

U.K	U.S.A	EUROPE
6	8	39
7	9	40
8	10	41
9	10.5	42
10	11	43
11	12	44
12	13	45

More useful conversions

1 centimetre	0.39 inches	1 inch	2.54 centimetres
1 metre	1.09 yards	1 yard	0.91 metres
1 kilometre	0.62 miles	1 mile	1. 61 kilometres
1 litre	1.76 pints	1 pint	0.57 litres
1 gram	0.35 ounces	1 ounce	28.35 grams
1 kilogram	2.2 pounds	1 pound	0.45 kilograms

This guide was written by **Katherine Vanderhaeghe**, with the assistance of **Charles Dierick** of the Musée de la Bande Dessinée, **Viviane Jacobs** of the Office de Promotion du Tourisme, **Franck Duval** master confectioner and **Jean-Pierre Van Roy** of the Brasserie Cantillon. Additional research and assistance **Claire Wedderburn-Maxwell**, **Sofi Mogensen**, **Christine Bell**, **Marie Barbelet**, **Caroline Boissy** and **Aurélie Joiris**. Translated by **Trista Selous** Project manager and copy editor **Margaret Rocques** Series editor **Liz Coghill**

We have done our best to ensure the accuracy of the information contained in this guide. However, addresses, phone numbers, opening times etc. inevitably do change from time to time, so if you find a discrepancy please do let us know. You can contact us at: hachetteuk@orionbooks.co.uk or write to us at Hachette UK, address below.

Hachette UK guides provide independent advice. The authors and compilers do not accept any remuneration for the inclusion of any addresses in these guides.

Please note that we cannot accept any responsibility for any loss, injury or inconvenience sustained by anyone as a result of any information or advice contained in this guide.

Photo acknowledgements

Inside pages
© **Éric Guillot**: pp. 2, 3, 10, 11, 12, 13 (t.; s. l.), 14 (b. l., reproduction rights), 15 (t.; b.), 16, 17, 18, 19, 20, 21 (b. l.), 22, 23 (t.; s. r.; b.), 24, 25 (b. l.), 26, 27, 28, 29, 31 (s. r.), 36, 37, 38, 39, 40, 41 (s. l.; m.; s. r.), 42, 43 (b. s.; t. s.), 44, 45, 46, 47, 48, 49 (s. l.; t. r.), 50 (b; m.; s. r.), 51, 52, 53 (t. s., b.l., b.r.), 54, 55, 56, 57, 58, 59, 60 (s. l.), 61, 62, 63, 67 (m.), 71 (t.; b.), 72, 75 (s. l.), 80 (t.), 82 (s. l.), 83 (t.; s. l.), 84 (t. r.; b. l.), 85 (t.; s. s.), 86 (t.; s. l.), 87 (s. l.; m.), 88, 89 (t. l; m.), 90, 91 (s. l.), 92, 93 (s. l.; s. r.; b.), 94, 95, 96 (b.), 97, 98 (m.; b.), 99 (m; b.), 100 (s. l.; m.; b.), 101, 102, 103, 104, 105, 106 (s. l; b.), 107, 109 (s. l; b.), 110 (t.; s. l.), 111 (m.; s. r.; b.), 112, 113 (s.l; s. r.), 116 (b.), 117 (s. l; b.), 120 (s. r.), 122 (b.), 123.
© **Laurent Parrault**: 82 (t.l.), 83 (s. r.), 85 (b.), 86 (s. r.), 87 (b. r.), 100 (t.), 108 (t.).
© **Christian Sarramon**: pp. 15 (s. r.), 21 (t.; s. r.), 23 (m.), 50 (t.), 111 (t.).
Hachette Livre: 14 (t.; m., reproduction rights), 24 (s. r.), 25 (b. r.).
Daniel Fouss: p. 13 (s. r.). **Delvaux**: p. 25 (s. l.), 30, 31 (b.), 109 (s. r.). **Ch. Bastin and I. Evrard**: p. 43 (t. l.). **Impasse St-Jacques**: p. 49 (b.). **Patricia Michaux, Apostrophes**: p. 53 (t.r.). **Autoworld**: p. 60 (s. l.). **Hôtel Amigo**: p. 66 (s. l.). **Hôtel Conrad**: p. 66 (s. r.). **Hôtel Les Bluets**: p. 67 (s. l.). **Hôtel Plaza**: p. 67 (s. r.). **Hôtel Palace**: p. 68 (t.). **Hôtel Stanhope**: p. 68 (s. r.). **Hôtel Astoria**: p. 68 (b.), 116 (s. r.). **Hôtel Montgoméry**: p. 69 (s. l.). **Céline Lambiotte**: p. 71 (t. r.). **Restaurant Inad**: p. 73 (s. l.). **Roger Begine**: p. 74 (t.). **Restaurant Les Bacchanales**: p. 74 (s. r.). **Restaurant Pasta Commedia**: p. 74 (s. l.). **Tea for Two**: p. 75 (b.). **Olivier Strelli**: p. 80 (s. l.; b.), 84 (t.), 87 (t. r.). **Elvis Pompilio**: p. 81 (s. r.). **Nicole Cadine**: p. 81 (s. l)) **Rue Blanche**: p. 82 (m.). **Johanna Riss**: p. 84 (s. r.). **Max and Lola**: p. 89 (b.). **Dujardin**: p. 89 (s. r.). **Linen House**: p. 91 (t.). **Dille & Kamille**: p. 93 (t.). **Dans la presse ce jour-là**: p. 96 (s.). **Au Fil du Temps**: p. 98 (t.), 99 (c. r.). **Hom**: p. 106 (b.). **Sabine Herman**: p. 108 (s.r.). **Côte à Côte**: p. 110 (s. r.). **Ambre Congo**: p. 113 (m.). **Théâtre Varia**: p. 117 (s. r.). **Jacques Debru**: p. 119 (b.).

Front cover
© **Eric Guillot**: T.l., t. r., m. l., s.r, b.l., b.r ; © **Stock Image** Nina Wolf: m.b.; **Stock Image** Peter Janssen: m; **Stock Image** P. Gueritot: t. m.; **Fotogram Stone**: s l.

Back cover
Eric Guillot

t: top; m.: middle; s.: side; r.: right; l.: left; b.: bottom

Illustrations: **Monique Prudent**

First published in the United Kingdom in 2000 by Hachette UK

© English Translation, revised and adapted, Hachette UK 2000
© Hachette Livre (Hachette Tourisme) 2000

All rights reserved. No part of this publication may be reproduced in any material form (including photocopying or storing it in any medium by electronic means and whether or not transiently or incidentally to some other use of this publication) without the written permission of the copyright owner, except in accordance with the provisions of the Copyright, Designs and Patents Act 1988 or under the terms of a licence issued by the Copyright Licensing Agency, 90 Tottenham Court Road, London W1P 9HE. Application for the copyright holder's permission to reproduce any part of this publication should be addressed to the publisher.

Distributed in the United States of America by Sterling Publishing Co., Inc. 387 Park Avenue South, New York, NY 10016-8810

A CIP catalogue for this book is available from the British Library

ISBN 1 84202 017 X

Hachette UK, Cassell & Co., The Orion Publishing Group, Wellington House, 125 Strand, London WC2R 0BB

Printed and bound in Italy by Milanostampa S.P.A.

If you're staying for a few days and would like to try some new places, the following pages give you a wide choice of hotels, restaurants (with addresses) listed by district and price (given in Belgian francs), and cafés where you can spend your evenings. Although you can just turn up at a restaurant and have a meal (except in the most prestigious establishments), don't forget to book your hotel several days in advance (see pages 66-69). Prices are a guide only. Enjoy your stay!

STAYING ON A LITTLE LONGER

Here's some good news: most hotels, particularly the 4- and 5-star establishments you'd expect to be much too expensive, offer big reductions (up to 50%) at weekends, ie Friday, Saturday and Sunday nights. These prices generally include breakfast. If not, you're better off having breakfast somewhere else, as it costs between BF400 and BF950. On the other hand, very few hotels offer free parking and there are very few free parking places in the city centre. Find out about this, as it's often cheaper to park your car in a public carpark than at your hotel. Some hotels, particularly the Accor chain, only offer reductions when they have a lot of vacancies. The prices given here are those that apply at weekends and during the months of July and August (double them for weekday prices) and hotels are classified according to the Belgium system. For more details see Rooms and Restaurants (p. 64).

Rogier/City Centre

Sheraton Brussels★★★★★
3, Place Rogier-1210
Metro: Rogier
☎ 224 3111
🖷 224 3456
BF5,100.
The largest hotel in Brussels with 587 rooms. It also has the highest altitude swimming-pool on the 30th floor with a lovely terrace, panoramic views and a gym. Very attentive service, quick check-out, access to the internet and Nintendo games via the TVs in the standard rooms (5th to 16th floor). These are very large with two double beds and a lovely bathroom. Live music in

the British-style Rendez-vous bar. There's an additional charge for use of the private car park.

Comfort Art Hotel Siru★★★★
2, Rue des Croisades-1210
Metro: Rogier
☎ 203 3580
🖷 203 3303
E-mail: art.hotel.siru@sky-net.be
BF3,200.
A lovely, comfortable hotel 15 minutes walk from Grand-Place. With unique works of contemporary art in each of the 101 rooms and in the corridors, it's a gallery with 130 Belgian artists for you to explore over your weekend. Includes Zulus by Wastijn and Deschuyme and Paul de Gobert's optical illusions.

Albert Premier★★★★
20, Place Rogier-1210
Metro: Rogier
☎ 203 3125
🖷 203 4331
BF3,500.
The beautiful old façade of white stone (1910) contrasts with the resolutely modernist interior. Basic decor and 287 good-size rooms, a bit cosier than it used to be. Ask for a room on the 8th or 9th floor with a view over the Botanic Gardens. Anglo-American-style buffet breakfast.

Hôtel des Colonies★★★
8-10, Rue des Croisades-1210
Metro: Rogier
☎ 203 3094
🖷 203 2944
From BF2,200 to BF2,900.
Ten minutes by metro from the Gare du Midi station, this Art Nouveau building (1908) was modified by American officers in 1945 and recently modernised to offer plenty of comfort and quiet. Its amazing mix of styles transports you to far-off places. Buffet breakfast is in an enormous room decorated with frescoes by Jean Fabry and you can use the car-park for an additional charge.

Daystar★★★
9, Square Victoria Regina-1210
Metro: Rogier

☎ 219 0661
🖷 219 3882
BF5,250.
Just near the Gare du Nord station, a Best Western hotel for lovers of American-style comfort. The 49 rooms are simply furnished, the breakfast buffet is very generous. Some parking places outside the hotel.

De Brouckère/Sainte-Catherine

Jolly Hotel Atlanta★★★★
7, Bd A. Max-1000
Metro: De Brouckère
☎ 217 0120
🖷 217 3758
BF4,200.
All that remains of the famous Art Deco Hotel Atlanta (1930) is the façade and the staircase. Redesigned by the Italian Jolly chain, it offers comfortable but rather dark rooms, a restaurant and a garage (for an additional charge of BF700) to travellers who want to stay in a central location.

Ibis – Sainte-Catherine★★★
2, Rue Joseph Plateau-1000
Metro: Sainte-Catherine
☎ 513 7620
🖷 513 7595
BF3,600, breakfast not included (BF300)
Typical of the style of this chain of hotels, it's cubic, functional and plastic with small standard rooms and tiny bathrooms. Good location in the fish restaurant quarter, with a public car park nearby.

Novotel – Tour Noire★★★
32, Rue de la Vierge Noire-1000
Metro: Sainte-Catherine
☎ 505 5050
🖷 505 5000
BF5,000, breakfast not included (BF500).
This pretentious building, opened in 1999, has swallowed up the Black Tower, one of the last remnants of the 11th-century city wall. It has the advantage of being located in a pleasant area and has spacious rooms, each with a double bed and sofa-bed. Gym, minimalist furniture and bathrooms, no private car park.

Vendôme★★★
98, Bd A. Max-1000
Metro: De Brouckère
☎ 227 0300
📠 218 0683
BF3,150
A large, grand and solid building which was renovated in 1995. It offers 116 well-equipped rooms with rattan furniture, buffet breakfast on the veranda and private garage (BF550).

Opéra★★
53, Rue Grétry-1000
Metro: De Brouckère
☎ 219 4343
📠 219 1720
BF2,700
Fifty simple but comfortable rooms decorated in shades of blue (no. 8 is the most pleasant), a good city centre location and a delicious breakfast. Public car park nearby.

Around Grand-Place

Radisson SAS★★★★★
47, Rue Fossé aux Loups-1000
Metro: Centrale
☎ 219 2828
📠 223 1818
Website:
www.radisson.com/brussels.be
From BF5,200
This hotel, built around a vast well of light, offers three types of room: Italian-style (leather and metal), oriental (rattan and flower prints) and Scandinavian (parquet floors and cool colours). You'll get maximum comfort in all of the 281 rooms, including the suites (junior or royal) which are at least twice as large and more expensive. Relaxation centre, star-rated restaurant (Sea Grill) and car park (BF770 additional charge).

Royal Windsor★★★★★
5, Rue Duquesnoy-1000
Metro: Centrale
☎ 505 5555
📠 505 5500
From BF4,500
(additional BF700 charge for breakfast)
All the luxury and refinement of a real grand hotel 100m/yds from Grand-Place. Attentive service round the clock, 266 tastefully decorated rooms and suites, direct telephone lines, gym and sauna. The speciality restaurant 'Les 4 Saisons' has a good wine list, and there's even a limousine service. Everything you need for a dream weekend. Additional charge for use of the garage (BF490).

Bedford★★★★
135, Rue du Midi-1000
Metro: Anneessens
☎ 512 7840
📠 514 1759
E-mail:
hotelbedford@pophost.eunet.be
BF3,600
Opposite the Academy of Art, this has been a reliable Brussels' hotel for over 40 years. Pleasant rooms, a warm welcome, large breakfast buffet and a piano bar and restaurant for those who are too tired to venture out of the hotel.

Aristote★★★
7, Av. de Stalingrad-1000
Metro: Anneessens
☎ 513 1310
📠 513 8070
BF2,800
This is a quiet hotel near Place Rouppe, has 25 modern, functional rooms, all with a bathroom. The rooms either overlook the boulevard or the courtyard at the back. There's a taverna with Italian-Belgian cuisine, buffet breakfast and there are some parking places in the area.

Novotel Brussels off Grand-Place★★★
120, Rue Marché aux Herbes -1000
Metro: Centrale
☎ 514 3333
📠 511 7723
BF5800
One of the hotels built in the imitation old style that disfigure the area around Grand-Place. In addition to its central location, it offers the basic comforts characteristic of all the Novotel hotels, which is most attractive to families due to the two extra beds in every room. Watch out for the hefty additional charges: breakfast BF500, public car park BF475.

HOTELS

À la Grande Cloche★★
10, Place Rouppe-1000
Metro: Anneessens
☎ 512 6 40
📠 512 6591
BF2,500

Ideally situated in a calm square 500m/yds from Grand-Place and opposite the best restaurant in Brussels. It has 45 rooms with a simple but adequate level of comfort (including 20 rooms with en-suite bathrooms). The 150 year-old building has historic significance. The French poet Rimbaud is said to have taken shelter here after being shot by Verlaine and the Nazis set up their HQ here. Breakfast in the old taverna and some parking places.

La Légende★★
35, Rue du Lombard-1000
Metro: Bourse
☎ 512 8290
📠 512 3493
From BF2,850

This is a simple hotel not far from the Mannekenpis, with different types of room. The most expensive and largest overlook the inner courtyard and the suite costs BF4,200. Belgian rolls for breakfast.

Sablon

Alfa Sablon★★★★
2-8, Rue de la Paille-1000
Bus: 48-Grand-Sablon
☎ 513 6040
📠 511 8141
E-mail: afla.sablon@alfa
hotels.com
BF3,900

All the friendliness of a small hotel with 32 rooms, all of which are different and very cosy, decorated in a style linked to the painters of the Cobra movement, many of whose works are on display. The corner rooms are larger and the duplex suites are ideal for families. Sauna, bar and very pleasant breakfast room. Some parking places in the street.

Jolly Hotel du Grand-Sablon★★★★
Place du Grand-Sablon-1000
Bus: 48-Grand-Sablon
☎ 512 8800
📠 512 6766
BF4,800

A new and comfortable hotel decorated in the Italian style with wood panelling, pale furniture and thick carpets. All the rooms have a little sitting-room and those with a double bed also have a jacuzzi. You'll have the choice of a room with a view over Place du Sablon (with the week-end antiques market) or a quieter room at the back. Additional charge of BF700 for the car park.

Louise

Hilton★★★★★
38, Bd de Waterloo-1000
Metro: Louise
☎ 504 1111
📠 504 2111
From BF5,600 to BF7,900

A sky-scraper with 27 floors, well placed between the Sablon antiques shops and the expensive shops of La Toison d'Or. It has 440 luxurious rooms with a panoramic view of the city and Egmont park. Very attentive service, particularly on the 'Executive and Business' floor. Brunch with a background of live jazz and the 'Maison du Bœuf' speciality restaurant.

Alfa Louise★★★★
212, Av. Louise-1050
Trams: 93/94-
Lesbroussart
☎ 644 2929
📠 644 1878
E-mail: alfa.louise@alfa-hotels.com
From BF5,100 to BF5,900

A stone's throw from the Art Nouveau gems designed by Horta, this is a small, modern hotel with 40 spacious rooms appointed with the services appropriate to their classification. Ask for a quiet room at the back for the view. Free use of the garage, which is very handy in this area.

Four Points★★★★
15, Rue Paul Spaak-1000
Tram: 93/94-
Lesbroussart
☎ 645 6111
📠 646 6344
From BF3,950 to BF4,350

Behind its façade of sombre brick, this hotel, recently taken over by the Sheraton group, has 128 impersonal rooms, with an additional charge of BF600 for a view over the garden.

It has two advantages: a relaxation centre with Turkish bath, sauna and jacuzzi and the copious breakfast buffet. Additional charge for use of the garage (BF390).

Holiday Inn★★★★
38, Chaussée de Charleroi-1060
Metro: Louise or tram: 91/92-Stéphanie
☎ 533 6666
📠 538 9014
BF3,900

Near Place Louise and its smart shops, this is a modern hotel with 200 luxurious rooms with all the services appropriate to the classification. Large underground garage (BF500).

Manos-Stéphanie★★★★
28, Chaussée de Charleroi-1060
Metro: Louise or tram: 91/92-Stéphanie
☎ 539 0250
📠 537 5729
BF4,000

An elegant mansion decorated with refined taste: crystal chandeliers, rich fabrics, Louis XVI-style furniture, gold leaf, marble and fresh flowers. One of the best hotels in Brussels where booking is essential as there are only 55 rooms. Generous morning buffet and private car park (BF250).

Chambord★★★
82, Rue de Namur -1000
Metro: Porte de Namur
☎ 548 9910
📠 514 0847
From BF2,700

Although this hotel has retained traces of its Art Deco period (lobby, staircase), the 70 rooms are decorated in the English country style. You'll have a choice of club class rooms, slightly larger business club class and the superb penthouse with a terrace on the 7th floor (BF6,000). Good value for money.

Beau-Site★★★
76, Rue de la Longue Haie-1050
Metro: Louise;
Bus: 54 - Vanne
☎ 640 8889
📠 640 1611
From BF2,500 to BF3,300

Pale shades combining wood and marble, a charming welcome and an ideal location in a quiet street just a stone's throw from Place Stéphanie and the expensive shops. The 38 very spacious rooms are worthy of a grand hotel and the variety and abundance of the breakfast buffet will set you up for a day spent walking round the city. Five parking places (BF250).

Cascade★★★★
128, Rue Berckmans-1060
Metro: Hôtel des Monnaies
☎ 538 8830
📠 538 9279
Double room from BF3,350 (weekend rate) to BF4,700
You'll get a generous breakfast and discreetly luxurious rooms in this fully-renovated grand hotel, well situated in the area containing all the restaurants, bars and shops. It's easy to get to from Gare du Midi station and also has an underground car park (additional charge of BF300 per night).

Gare du Midi

Ustel★★★
6-8, Square de l'Aviation-1070
Metro: Lemonnier
☎ 520 6028
📠 520 3328
BF3,000
This red-brick building dating from 1870, is in a former industrial area which is currently being renovated. It has 94 modern rooms, an attentive welcome and breakfast on the garden terrace at the back. The trendy restaurant is located in part of the vaults for the underground river Senne. Private car park (BF300).

Quartier Léopold (EU)

Leopold Brussels★★★★
35, Rue du Luxembourg-1050
Rail: Quartier Léopold-
Metro: Trône
☎ 511 1828
📠 514 1939
From BF2,900 (additional charge of BF400 for breakfast)
A neo-Classical building in an area which is quiet despite its

location near the upper end of the city. Patronised by Eurocrats during the week and excellent value for money at weekends. Cosy and comfortable with a speciality restaurant 'Les Anges' (set meal at BF1,395), lovely terrace and some parking places in the street and car park (BF300).

A little further out

Winston★★★
98, Rue de Stalle-1180
Tram: 91-Stalle
☎ 376 3535
📠 332 1449
BF3,500
A patrician house dating from 1920, close to the Drogenbos motorway exit, with nine pretty and individualised rooms. There's a family welcome, a red suite with a private terrace (BF4,500), a garden terrace where you can have your breakfast, free parking and leafy surroundings, not to mention 'Les Proverbes' restaurant, a favourite with the residents of Uccle.

It's hard to find a good restaurant that's open on a Sunday. However, the list below gives a selection of addresses that will at least prevent you from starving. Remember most of the grand hotels serve classic, refined, but sometimes expensive cuisine every day. They eat quite late in Brussels, particularly at weekends, and prices are fairly high, especially if you decide to order a bottle of good wine.

Around Grand-Place

Armand & Ko
16 Rue des Chapeliers-1000
☎ 514 1763
Open every day lunchtimes and evenings
About BF1,200.
In this 16th-century building in a narrow street near the Grand-Place, a collection of advertisements on enamel plaques are the high points of the decor. As for the food, it's mainly traditional seasonal fare with a dish of the day at BF395. Classic dishes include stuffed roast beef with spinach and pig's foot feuillantine.

Chez Vincent
8 Rue des Dominicains-1000
☎ 511 2607
Open every day lunchtime and evening
BF1,000-1,500.
Although it's always full of tourists, this restaurant, decorated with an immense fresco, is still one of the best places to eat mussels with chips. Warm, friendly atmosphere guaranteed.

La Cigogne
78 Rue A. Dansaert-1000
Metro: Bourse
☎ 502 8742
Closed Sun.-Mon.
Dishes BF300/400.
Claude Remy is the man behind the revival of this old Eetcafé, literally a café where you can eat. It has wooden seats where you squeeze up to enjoy authentic

family cooking made from fresh ingredients. The short menu changes twice a day and there's something to suit every taste: meat, fish and vegetables, and you can even order your favourite dish.

Plattesteen
41 Rue Marché au Charbon-1000
☎ 512 8203.
This authentic Brussels' eatery, a stone's throw from Grand-Place, serving unpretentious cuisine (dish of the day at BF340) accompanied by wine or good Belgian beers, has still not really been discovered by the tourists. A stamcafé (local) full of theatrical types and rockers, it also has a large sunny terrace (in summer).

Rugantino
184-186 Bd Anspach-1000
☎ 511 2195
Closed Sat. lunchtimes and Sun.
About BF1,400.
You'll find a mixed crowd on the balcony and inside this establishment where, for the last 25 years, Antonio and Constantina have served delicious Italian cuisine based on olive oil. You absolutely must try their superb antipasti, pizzas, dishes of the day and zabaglione.

Samouraï
28 Rue Fossé aux Loups-1000
Metro: De Brouckère
☎ 217 5639
Closed Sun. lunchtimes and Tue.
Set meals BF1,500-2,500.
One of the best Japanese restaurants in Brussels, frequented by many celebrities, who've written dedications full of praise. The chef's secret is to offer local produce (foie gras, asparagus, chicory) cooked in Japanese style along with the classic shashimi, sushi and tempura. Everything is fresh, the service is perfect and there's a very good list of French wines.

Scheltema
7 Rue des Dominicains-1000
☎ 512 2084
Lunchtimes and evenings; closed Sun.
About BF2,000.

Near Rue des Bouchers, this brasserie specialising in shellfish and seafood dishes is one of the few good restaurants in the area. Specialities include fish soup and salmon with orange.

Marolles

Au Sterkerlapatte
4 Rue des Prêtres-1000
Open every evening except Mon.
Set meals from BF1,050.
Hidden in the depths of Marolles, this is one of the most authentic of Brussels' restaurants, frequented primarily by artists and journalists. Crammed in together on wooden seats, you can eat bloempanch with apples, braised chicory, pheasant à la brabançonne or rabbit with gueuse beer – invigorating Belgian dishes accompanied by good beer or French wine. Booking essential.

Les Petits Oignons
13 Rue Notre Seigneur-1000
☎ 512 4738
Lunchtimes and evenings, closed Sun.
Set meals from BF950.
A building decorated with flowers, an exceptional garden and a warm welcome from the Zoughlamis. Classic French cuisine including snails, calf's brains, foie gras terrine and champagne. Wines to match.

Vismet (Sainte-Catherine)

François
13 Place Sainte-Catherine-1000
☎ 511 6089
Lunchtimes and evenings, closed Mon.
BF2,000-2,500.
The bistrot where they used to serve fried fish has evolved along with the generations born to François Veulemans. It has become a high-class fish restaurant serving extremely refined dishes such as lobster.

Rugbyman N°1
4 Quai aux Briques-1000
☎ 512 5640
Open every day lunchtimes and evenings
Set meal BF1,495.

This restaurant with its plush interior has specialised in preparing lobster for more than half a century. Most pleasant when the terrace is open. Traditional fish and some meat dishes. Shame the welcome is so unfriendly.

Quartier Louise

Bistrot du Mail
81 Rue du Mail-1050
☎ 539 0697
Closed Sat. lunchtime and Sun.
Far from being a bistrot, this excellent restaurant is well-known to the locals. Plain Belgian-French cuisine with the emphasis on freshness and taste, whether you're eating fish from the market or traditional steak accompanied by a bottle of good wine.

Café Camille
559 Chaussée de Waterloo-1050
☎ 345 9643
Closed Sat. and Sun. lunchtimes
About BF1,500.
The lovely brasserie decor and good French cuisine are attracting more and more trendy types (and their mobile phones), to the dismay of the regular customers of this fine restaurant near the Art Nouveau quarter. The tables are snatched up for lunch (BF325), particularly when the pavement terrace is open.

Le Fils de Jules
35-37 Rue du Page-1050
☎ 534 0057
Closed Sat. and Sun. lunchtimes
Set meal BF1,300, including wine.
If you're counting the calories, you'd better keep walking. The specialities from the Basque country and the French Landes region, served in a sober decor of wood and black marble, are far from minimalist. Foie gras, confit of duck, and other wonderfully tempting creations including divine desserts such as crème brûlée and chocolate fondant.

Fin de Siècle
423 Av. Louise-1050
☎ 648 8041
Closed Sat. lunchtime and Sun.
About BF1,600.

Silver, crystal, family pictures and Baroque music give atmosphere to this lovely restaurant on Avenue Louise. A refined setting where you can enjoy Italian cuisine to match. In summer the garden adds to the attractions.

Tutto Pepe
123 Rue Faider-1050
☎ 534 9619
Closed Sat. lunchtime and Sun.
Two microscopic rooms whose decor evokes the spice route from the East. Mainly Italian cuisine, with an emphasis on pasta and classics like antipasto (BF700), minestra (BF320) and tagliata di vitello on a bed of rucola (BF640). Delicious food, but the bill is less easy to digest!

Around Place Flagey

L'Heure Douze
50 Chaussée de Vleurgat-1050
☎ 640 4560
Closed Sat. lunchtime and Sun.
Speciality menu BF850.
An intimate place filled with clocks where they serve delicious French specialities in season. A warm welcome, large portions, pleasant garden and the chef's own pastries fill you with delight. Good value for money.

Mieux Vaut Boire Ici Qu'en Face
40 Rue A. De Witte-1050
☎ 644 3031
Lunchtimes and evenings, closed Sun.
About BF1,000.
Opposite the church on Place Flagey, with a rich purple decor, authentic French country cooking including great classic dishes and a superb wine list (350 types) selected by Daniel Marcil from Quebec, now Brussels' foremost wine steward.

Uccle

Les Brasseries Georges
259 Av. Winston Churchill-1180
☎ 347 2100
Lunchtimes and evenings, closed Sun.
About BF1,800.

RESTAURANTS

This noisy place with its highly charged atmosphere is the brasserie of businessmen and Uccle residents. An impressive oyster bar and brasserie food, from sauerkraut to steamed cod. It's good, a bit expensive and always very busy.

Ce Soir on Dîne à Marrakech
408 Av. Brugmann-1180
☎ 347 7601
Lunchtime and evenings, closed Mon.
BF1,000-1,500, lunch BF350 .
This fine mansion has been transformed into a Berber house, serving traditional cuisine of the Middle Atlas region. The marrakechia table, with its assortment of hot entrées, royal couscous and pastilla with milk and orange flower is superb. Moroccan wines and a garden open in fine weather.

Ventre Saint-Gris
10 Rue Basse-1180
☎ 375 2755
Open every day lunchtimes and evenings.
The highly refined decor and delightful summer garden in this expensive district of Brussels are in tune with the inventive and flavoursome French cuisine. Lobster farandole, hot apple tart, speculoos ice-cream and a set meal at BF795, which changes every fortnight.

Around Place Schuman (EEC)

Balthazar
63 Rue Archimède-1000
☎ 742 0600
Closed Sat. lunchtime and Sun.
About BF1,500.
A surprising setting of columns and wood-panelling (and a garden) for very inventive Mediterranean-style cuisine. Mezze with good olive oil, fresh salads and fish grilled to perfection. Perfect service too and a very fair price in the district favoured by the Eurocrats.

L'Esprit de Sel
52 Place Jourdain-1040
☎ 230 6040
Closed Sat. lunchtime and Sun.
Set meal from BF895.

Calligraphy and chandeliers in this rich, intimate setting where you can enjoy original recipes by a talented young chef at very reasonable prices. A favourite haunt of ministers, artists and the inhabitants of Brussels in general.

TRENDY RESTAURANTS

Bonsoir Clara
22-26 Rue Antoine Dansaert-1000
☎ 502 0990
Closed Sat. and Sun. lunchtimes
About BF1,200.
Coloured glass mosaics adorn the walls and the bay windows open onto the down-town passersby. Fashionable quick cuisine: vitello tonnato, carpaccio or rabbit à la grand-mère.

Le Living Room
50 Chaussée de Charleroi-1060
☎ 534 4434
Open every day lunchtimes and evenings
About BF2,000.
With Cerberus at the door, and ultra-cool serving staff, this is the new in-vogue eatery with an eclectic, colourful decor. The hyper-trendy world-brasserie menu guarantees a large bill. If you want to catch a glimpse of anyone who's anyone in Brussels, this is the place to come.

Lola
33, Place du Grand-Sablon-1000
☎ 514 2460
Open every day lunchtimes and evenings
About BF1,600.
Minimalist stainless steel and wood decor for contemporary cuisine somewhere between local dishes and a lighter Mediterranean style. Very busy, mainly good and fairly expensive.

La Manufacture
12, Rue Notre-Dame du Sommeil-1000
☎ 502 2525
Closed Sat lunchtime and Sun.
About BF1,800.
A rather chilly setting of the old Delvaux leather workshops and a slightly pretentious Japanese-

influenced cuisine, accompanied by wines from around the world. Patrons are more interested in being seen than tasting the food.

Le Majestic
33, Rue du Magistrat-1050
☎ 639 1330
Noon-midnight, closed Sun.
About BF1,500.
A wild decor of giant spangles in sulphurous colours singles out this restaurant-café-bar. The cosmopolitan clientele are offered a choice of colourful food from around the world. Slimmers menus, organic dishes, brunch 11.30am to 3pm at BF950, bar open until 3am.

HAUTE CUISINE

Bruneau
75 Av. Broustin-1083 Ganshoren
☎ 427 6978
Closed Tue. evening and Wed.
BF4,500 a head.
In Brussels Jean-Pierre Bruneau shares three stars with Pierre Wynants. Sober decor and technology set the food off to best effect: lobster rosette with truffles, fillet of sea bass, calf's sweetbreads stuffed with truffles and celery ravioli with truffles.

Comme Chez Soi
23 Place Rouppe-1000
☎ 512 2921
Lunchtimes and evenings, closed Sun. and Mon.
BF4,500 a head.
Cuisine and service fit for a king in Pierre Wynant's restaurant, whose reputation has long spread beyond Belgium's borders. You have to book months in advance to taste the émincé of poultry with scallops and truffles, the fillet of sole with riesling mousseline and shrimps and the hare façon bécasse.

Claude Dupont
46 Av. Vital Riethuisen-1083 Ganshoren
☎ 426 0000
Lunchtimes and evenings, closed Mon. and Tue.
Set meal from BF1,775.
A discreet establishment near the Kœkelberg Basilica where Claude Dupont offers a refined, light

cuisine. Try the eel and smoked salmon mousse, the Colchester oysters au gratin with champagne, the venison with thyme and the praline chaud-froid.

L'Écailler du Palais Royal
18 Rue Bodenbroeck-1000
☎ 512 8751
Lunchtimes and evenings, closed Sun.
À la carte menu:
BF3,500-4000.
The best fish restaurant, run by Attilio Basso. Delicious sea urchin soufflé, scallop salad with truffles and North Sea bouillabaisse.

Sea Grill
47 Rue Fossé-aux-Loups-1000
☎ 217 9225
Closed Sat. lunchtime and Sun.
Set meal at BF2,550 changes every month.
Chef Yves Mattagne, awarded two stars by the Michelin guide, has a fine menu of seafood specialities, including bluefin tuna tartare, roast turbot and royal crab from the Barents Sea accompanied by risotto with black truffles. The desserts are equally mouthwatering, especially the crème brûlée.

L'Alban Chambon
21 Place de Brouckère-1000
☎ 217 7650
Lunchtimes and evenings, closed Sat.-Sun.
À la carte menu:
BF1,500-2,800.
The Belle Époque decor of the Hôtel Métropole complements the refined cuisine by Dominique Michou, who offers turbot soufflé with lobster, creamed cod, pheasant with chicory and custard tart with caramelised apples. On Wednesdays you can even bring your own wine to drink.

BRUNCH

Atrium
47 Rue Fossé aux-loups-1000
☎ 227 31701
11.30am-2.30pm.
Scandinavian and Belgian specialities served in the pleasant central courtyard of the Hôtel
SAS, with the Atriumvira Quartet playing in the background (Bach, Ravel, Brahms, Mozart, Verdi etc.).

En Plein Ciel
38 Bd de Waterloo-1000
☎ 504 2800
10am-3pm.
Brunch in style on the 27th floor of the Hilton. For BF1,690 you can have champagne, hors d'oeuvres, a hot buffet, a choice of desserts and live jazz from the Roger Vanha Trio.

Het Warme Water
19 Rue des Renards-1000
☎ 513 9159
7.30am-5pm.
An Eetcafé in the heart of Marolles where you can eat couques and open plattekaas sandwiches and have a lively political discussion over a pot of coffee. The place to meet up with friends on a Sunday after bargain-hunting on Place du Jeu de Balle.

Crescendo Bar (Sheraton)
3 Place Rogier-1210
☎ 224 3111
11am-3pm.
If you feel like diving into the lovely 30th floor swimming pool before sampling the wonders of the buffet brunch, it's all yours for BF1,350, including cloakroom service. Really relaxing.

WITH LIVE MUSIC

La Voix Secrète
1 Rue du Lombard-1000
☎ 511 5679
Open 7pm-3pm, summer 3pm-2am, closed Mon.
This dark, modern-medieval café-restaurant is a showcase for unknown artists, with a varied repertoire that attracts an enthusiastic, cosmopolitan crowd. Light but luxurious meals served late into the night (dishes BF500 max.).

Le Siècle
41 Rue de l'Ecuyer-1000
☎ 513 0810
Set meals: BF990, 1290, 1490.
Reminiscent of Club 18-30. Noisy groups, music mixed by the DJ, theme nights (VIPs, singles, striptease, gay, Ibiza etc.). Sound level rises as the night progresses.

RESTAURANTS

CAFÉS

À la Mort Subite
7 Rue Montagne-aux-
Herbes Potagères-1000
☎ 513 1318
Mon.-Sat. 10.30-1am,
Sun. 12.30pm-1am.
*A long, smoke-filled room and
wooden seats, a real 'brown café'
like in Amsterdam where they
mainly drink specialities of
Brussels: lambic, gueuze and
faro.*

Blue Note
32 Rue Defacqz-1050
☎ 539 0502 or
075 69 3631
Open every day from 4pm.
*Named after the famous record
label, Blue Note has good
Chicago jazz every evening in the
district of bars often frequented
by lone businessmen.*

Conway's
10 Avenue de la Toison
d'Or-1000
☎ 502 2910
Open every night 6pm-
1am.
*Highly charged atmosphere and
Saturday night fever in this
American bar where they eat
hamburgers and cheesecake
accompanied by bourbon and
tequila before dancing on the
bar. Should be experienced at
least once if you can get through
the door.*

Le Grain de Sable
15-16 Place du Grand-
Sablon-1000
☎ 514 0583
Open every day 9-2am.
*Perfect for seeing and being
seen, preferably with your mobile
phone and convertible, for before
or after dinner or, best of all, on
Sunday after a trip round the
antique shops.*

Jacqmotte Coffee House
37 Grand-Place-1000
☎ 551 0319
Mon.-Thu. 9am-7pm, Fri
and Sun. 9am-10pm, Sat.
9am-midnight.
*The modern interior contrasts
with the Baroque-rustic style
of the neighbouring cafés.
With its contemporary, not to
say futuristic decor, this is the*
home of freshly-ground coffee
for your breakfast or your afternoon break.

Mappa Mundo
2-6 Rue du Pont de la
Carpe-1000
☎ 514 3555
Open every day 8-3am.
*A huge map of the world painted
on the façade and music drifting
out from the mullioned windows
tempt passersby. The sign
isn't that necessary as this has
become the popular new meeting
place for trendy types. It's doing
very well despite the surly staff.
Pavement terrace in summer.*

Moeder Lambic
68 Rue de Savoie-1060
Mon.-Sat. 11-4am, Sun.
4pm-3am.
*A café for fans of beer (an
impressive list) and comics,
which are available to customers.
A good old stamcafé.*

Mokafé
9 Galerie du Roi-1000
☎ 511 7870
Mon.- Sat. 8-1am, Sun.
10-1am.
*With its promenade terrace
beneath the glass roof of the
Galerie Saint-Hubert and its
decor which has remained
unchanged since 1847, this is
the meeting-place of old ladies
at tea time and a cosmopolitan
crowd in the early evening.*

De Ultieme Hallucinatie
316 Rue Royale-1210
☎ 217 0614
Open every day 11-3am.
*Behind a room in the purest Art
Nouveau style, this is a kind of
station waiting-room à la Delvaux
with a long bar where the ticket
office would have been. A marvellous place to spend an evening
chatting over a selection from the
list of beers.*

BARS

DNA
20 Plattesteen-1000
☎ 513 6860
Open every night 8pm-
2/3am.
*After the new wave and punk
eras, the clientele has calmed
down a bit but the combined*
decibel level of the motorbikes
outside and rock music inside
remains just as high. Speciality of
the house is iced vodka.

Goupil Le Fol
22 Rue de la Violette-
1000
☎ 511 1396
Open every night 8pm-
5am.
*Good old Abdel, who's in love
with the Belgian royal dynasty
and French chanson, always
serves cocktails of his own
devising to sip in the battered
armchairs on the different floors
of this rambling old house, decorated with candles and stripy
vinyl.*

New York Café
5 Chaussée de Charleroi-
1060
☎ 534 8509
Thu.-Sat. 6pm-4am.
*Red velvet, red carpet and
Marilyn Monroe's smile. A very
glamourous setting for a drink
and a hamburger or chili con
carne before dancing to house,
disco and remixed hits. Clientele
mainly Americans and expats.*

Zen
77 Rue du Page-1050
☎ 538 9931
Mon.-Fri. 11-3am, Sat.
6pm-2am.
*A local bar with a trendy interior
for hip 20 to 30-year-olds.
Good music, spirits at BF170
and deluxe cigars.*

CLUBS

Tour et Taxis
5 Rue Picard-1000
☎ 420 5505
Fri.-Sat. 11pm-8am; entry
BF300 after midnight.
*An off-beat, loft-style interior and
house music for a mainly young
clientele. World music gigs and
performances during the annual
'Couleur café' festival in the last
week of June.*

Le Bal
47 Bd du Triomphe-1160
☎ 649 3500
Fri.-Sat. 11pm-5am.
*Local dance-type atmosphere
with paper lanterns. Patronised
mainly by students.*

Le Strong
17 Rue du Pinçon-1000
☎ 511 9398.
Gay club. For men only, every Sunday.

BARS/CAFÉS

EXCURSIONS IN THE SURROUNDING AREA

Butte du Lion at Waterloo (via the East ringroad)

To see the panorama of the famous battle of 18 June 1815, climb up the Butte or mound (226 steps) at Braine l'Alleud or visit the Wellington Museum at Waterloo (☎ 354 7806; 9.30am-6.30pm in summer and 10.30am-5pm in winter). This was Wellington's HQ and contains a few of his personal items. To find out more about Napoleon's defeat and details of the battle as it progressed, this is well worth a visit.

Château de Gaasbeek

A medieval building with a drawbridge and dungeon perched on a hill in the middle of Pajottenland. At the bottom of the hill you'll find an inn where you can sample country-style omelettes or bread and cream-cheese with gueuse beer.

SOME LITTLE GEMS TO VISIT

Chinese Pavillon and Japanese Tower

44 Av. Van Praet-1020 Laeken
Trams: 19/23/32/92
☎ 268 1608
Tue.-Sun. 10am-4.30pm.
Near the royal residence of the Château de Laeken (not open to the public) you'll find two follies dating from 1900, erected by King Leopold II: the Japanese Tower, entirely laquered in dark red with superb exotic stained glass designed by J. Galland, and the Chinese Pavillon, containing a display of fine Chinese porcelain and furniture. In the cemetery behind Laeken church there are some fine funerary monuments including a copy of Rodin's Thinker.

Royal Museum of Central Africa in Tervuren

13 Leuvensesteenweg-3080
☎ 769 5211
Tue.-Fri. 10am-5pm;
Sat.-Sun. 10am-6pm.
Beneath its great glass roof the former Congo Museum at the terminus of tram no 44 contains one of the finest collections of African art, mostly originating from the Democratic Republic of Congo, formerly a Belgian colony. The grounds are superb.

Dieweg cemetery in Uccle

Tram: 18/92- Dieweg
Intertwining branches and wild flowers, knotted roots pushing up the slabs, mysterious sphinxes and pillars, this abandoned cemetery, with its wild beauty, is the last resting place of Hergé and many Belgian Jewish families.

FURTHER AFIELD

NOTES

HACHETTE TRAVEL GUIDES

Titles available in this series:

A GREAT WEEKEND IN AMSTERDAM (ISBN: 1 84202 002 1)
A GREAT WEEKEND IN BARCELONA (ISBN: 1 84202 005 6)
A GREAT WEEKEND IN FLORENCE (ISBN: 1 84202 010 2)
A GREAT WEEKEND IN LONDON (ISBN: 1 84202 013 7)
A GREAT WEEKEND IN NAPLES (ISBN: 1 84202 016 1)
A GREAT WEEKEND IN NEW YORK (ISBN: 1 84202 004 8)
A GREAT WEEKEND IN PARIS (ISBN: 1 84202 001 3)
A GREAT WEEKEND IN PRAGUE (ISBN: 1 84202 000 5)
A GREAT WEEKEND IN ROME (ISBN: 1 84202 003 X)
A GREAT WEEKEND IN BERLIN (ISBN: 1 84202 061 7)
A GREAT WEEKEND IN BRUSSELS (ISBN: 1 84202 017 X)
A GREAT WEEKEND IN VIENNA (ISBN: 1 84202 026 9)

Publication Autumn 2000
A GREAT WEEKEND IN VENICE (ISBN: 1 84202 018 8)

HACHETTE VACANCES
Who better to write about France than the French?
A series of colourful, information-packed, leisure and activity guides for family holidays by French authors. Literally hundreds of suggestions for things to do and sights to see per title.

BRITTANY (ISBN: 1 84202 007 2)
LANGUEDOC-ROUSSILLON (ISBN: 1 84202 008 0)
POITOU-CHARENTES (ISBN: 1 84202 009 9)
PROVENCE & THE COTE D'AZUR (ISBN: 1 84202 006 4)
PYRENEES & GASCONY (ISBN: 1 84202 015 3)
SOUTH-WEST FRANCE (ISBN: 1 84202 014 5)

ROUTARD
Comprehensive and reliable guides offering insider advice for the independent traveller, starting autumn 2000.

ANDALUCIA (ISBN: 1 84202 028 5)
BELGIUM (ISBN: 1 84202 022 6)
BRITTANY (ISBN: 1 84202 020 X)
CALIFORNIA, NEVADA & ARIZONA (ISBN: 1 84202 025 0)
CUBA (ISBN: 1 84202 062 5)
GREEK ISLANDS & ATHENS (ISBN: 1 84202 023 4)
IRELAND (ISBN: 1 84202 024 2)
PARIS (ISBN: 1 84202 027 7)
PROVENCE & THE COTE D'AZUR (ISBN: 1 84202 019 6)
SOUTHERN ITALY, ROME & SICILY (ISBN: 1 84202 021 8)
THAILAND (ISBN: 1 84202 029 3)
WEST CANADA & ONTARIO (ISBN: 1 84202 031 5)